# The Names of GOD

## by Marilyn Hickey

Marilyn
Hickey
Ministries

P.O. Box 17340
Denver, Colorado 80217

# THE NAMES OF GOD

ISBN 1-56441-014-5

Unless otherwise indicated, all Scripture quotations are taken from the *King James Version* of the Bible.

# CONTENTS

*Dear Friend,*

*In Isaiah 33:6, the prophet declared, "And wisdom and knowledge shall be the stability of thy times, . . . ." That scripture is as applicable today as it was when Isaiah first spoke it concerning the sins that plagued Judah centuries ago.*

*Today, the threat of murder, terrorism, and nuclear "mishaps" dominates our newspaper and television headlines and tries to instill fear in our hearts. It's comforting to know that God has promised to provide stability in these precarious times through knowledge and wisdom.*

*But how does God reveal His knowledge to us? Primarily through His Word. And one of the most meaningful ways He reveals Himself to us is through His names. Each of God's glorious names reveals dynamic dimensions and miraculous characteristics of His awesome power and endless love for us. Through studying His names and their meanings, we can learn the keys to tapping into His infinite supply of energy and find stability during even the most adverse situations.*

*I know that as you begin your study on the names of God, He will reveal Himself to you in a most intimate and personal way and His glory will be reflected in your life.*

*His love and mine,*

Marilyn Hickey

# Chapter One

# ELOHIM

**E**LOHIM is the very first title of God that you encounter in the Bible:

> *"In the beginning God created the heaven and the earth"* (Genesis 1:1).

The Hebrew translation for the name GOD is actually EL, or ELOHIM. Fascinating in its translation, this name is one of God's more frequently occurring titles; it shows up over 2,500 times in the Bible! It must be important that we understand its meaning.

EL is the root word of ELOHIM, and it describes God's greatness and glory; it displays God's power and sovereignty. Although this word is comprised of only two letters, it offers a glimpse into the depth of the Hebrew language—a language of pictures.

Consider the name ELOHIM, which extends the scope of EL's root meaning. ELOHIM brings forth a new dimension to the God of power: He becomes the God Who creates! Thus far two facets of God make up the word ELOHIM: (1) total power and might and complete sovereignty; and (2) complete creativity.

Notice that in the Bible's very first verse, God was shown as the Creator! In using the name ELOHIM, Genesis 1:1 makes the statement that tremendous, unimaginable power is involved in the force of God's creativity. ELOHIM, in His mighty power and creativity, caused our vast universe to exist:

> *Through faith we understand that the worlds were framed by the word of God, so that things which are seen were not made of things which do appear* (Hebrews 11:3).

God's name, ELOHIM, is amazing in itself, but it bears another striking characteristic that makes it even more distinctive: the Hebrew ending for ELOHIM is plural! Why? Because it describes the divine trinity of the Godhead—Father, Son, and Holy Spirit. No singular word could describe this element of God's personality.

Several places throughout the Bible confirm this plurality. Genesis 1 says this about the creation of the first man, Adam:

> *And God said, Let us make man in our image, after our likeness: . . . So God created man in his own image, in the image of God created he him; male and female created he them* (Genesis 1:26,27).

God the Father, Jesus the Son, and the Holy Spirit were all involved in the powerful creative process that occurred upon the earth. Genesis 1 shows that the Holy Spirit was present:

> *". . . And the Spirit of God moved upon the face of the waters. And God said, 'Let there be light:' and there was light"* (Genesis 1:2-3).

Why was the Holy Spirit moving upon the face of the waters? Because He was preparing to create!

Jesus was actively involved in the creation process too:

> *For by him were all things created, that are in heaven, and that are in earth, visible and invisible, whether they be thrones, or dominions, or principalities, or powers: all things were created by him, and for him* (Colossians 1:16).

Active, present, full of creative power: Elohim! Father, Son, and Holy Spirit. This increases the impact of Jesus' shocking statement to the religious men of His day: "Before Abraham was, I Am." What an exciting, infinite personality!

I like this analogy: God is the Architect; Jesus is the Builder; and the Holy Spirit is He Who breathes the life of God into the structure. ELOHIM: THOSE Who are mighty and powerful; THOSE Who are creative and sovereign.

Yet, there is another facet to ELOHIM, making Him an active part of His creation. It is ELOHIM Who makes covenants with those whom He created! Later, you will study the name JEHOVAH, the name in which God reveals His ways. ELOHIM is the name in which God reveals His power. It is this very power and creativity that allows God Himself to enter into covenant relationship with you and me.

The apostle Paul had a revelation of ELOHIM:

> *For I am not ashamed of the gospel of Christ: for it is the power of God unto salvation to everyone that believeth; to the Jew first, and also to the Greek* (Romans 1:16).

Paul said, "God's covenant of salvation with you and me is His power!" Don't ever speak lightly of the gospel—God's covenant with us, because that is His power that gave us eternal life; His power that saved us now and forever! Our covenant-making ELOHIM sustains all that He created through His own might. Throughout Genesis, whenever God created, He spoke first, then manifested His power.

Naturally, ELOHIM loved His creation, and He desired to preserve it. Although God was protective toward the people of His creation, they seemed only to get better and better at being worse and worse! And as the people sinned, they separated themselves further away from their Creator. God is merciful, but He is also holy and righteous. Sin was (and still is) offensive to Him, and something had to be done before these people destroyed themselves. ELOHIM observed that this growing sinfulness spread like cancer through each successive generation.

As man continued in this downhill pattern, God began to notice a man named Enoch. Enoch wasn't outstanding in his hunger for God, and his life was fairly uneventful until he reached age 65. But then something happened that turned his life around: Enoch's wife bore a child, and God told Enoch, "Name that baby **Methuselah**," which means, "I've had enough of this sinfulness, so when that child dies, the flood will come upon the earth."

Surely no child received the tender loving care that Methuselah received! Enoch lived in a day that was devoid of modern medicine. Death was a frequent visitor, and it often claimed the lives of small babies and children who lacked resistance to disease. You can imagine Enoch's shock: "If this baby dies, the deluge will come and totally destroy the earth. Take good care of him!"

Something began to happen within Enoch's heart as he cared for Methuselah: Enoch began to respond to his Creator. During the next 300 years, Enoch cultivated his relationship with God. Finally something really tremendous happened:

*"And Enoch walked with God: and he was not; for God took him"* (Genesis 5:24).

One day Enoch was going about his usual routine, increasing

11

in faith, when suddenly, God just reached down and carried him out of this life and into life eternal! **To translate** means "to carry across." Hebrews 11:5 says that Enoch was translated by faith! Meanwhile, Methuselah was still alive, growing older, probably keeping people on pins and needles. The people knew the day was coming when the floods would arrive.

Although Enoch had been walking closely with God, the same thing can't be said about the other people in his generation. Their sinfulness vexed God continually; yet Methuselah lived longer than any other person recorded in the Bible—969 years! His life was tremendously long for one reason: God kept extending His mercy and grace, because He hoped to preserve His creation! He loved those people, and He did not want to destroy them.

Methuselah had a child named Lamech, and one of his sons was Noah. Notice the family line: when you enter into a covenant with God, His promises are also made to your children and each successive generation of your family. One day God spoke to Noah:

> " . . .'The end of all flesh is come before me; for the earth is filled with violence through them; and, behold, I will destroy them with the earth'" (Genesis 6:13).

God proceeded to give Noah directions for building the ark, and Noah obeyed. Over the years, people began to take God's warning for granted. I would have thought that when Noah started building, they'd have said, "Oh no! Methuselah's dead, and God is going to send that flood He warned us about!" But the people reacted totally differently than expected—they scoffed at Noah. They'd had almost 1,000 years to repent. Noah preached continually about God's intentions, but people still rebelled. God always warns His people ahead when judgment is coming. He wants to give everyone a chance to repent first.

One day as I was picturing Noah in my mind as he built the huge ark, the Lord began to reveal Noah's faith to me. Noah had tremendous faith! Especially considering the fact that rain had never before fallen upon the earth!

Noah built that ark to comply with God's specifications, and it took 120 years to accomplish it. Just imagine having people harass you for that long! He had every physical reason to stop in the eightieth year and say, "I've had enough of building this ark while everybody else laughs! God, this is ridiculous—I mean, I've never even seen rain before, and here You have me preaching that there's going to be a flood! I quit!" But Noah didn't give up; instead, he confidently held on to God's Word and continued to build the ark:

> *Cast not away therefore your confidence, which hath great recompence of reward. For ye have need of patience, that, after ye have done the will of God, ye might receive the promise* (Hebrews 10:35-36).

Noah received a big reward for his patience—he had finished the will of God! He and his family were spared, and the seed parts of the earth were saved, so that it, too, could be replenished.

When God calls you to accomplish something, don't quit! God could have said, "I've had it; I'm destroying this whole earth!" But He didn't say that. Noah could have quit very easily—but he didn't. And you should never give up either—

you have been created in God's image, and God never quits!

After having accomplished God's will, Noah and his family were spared. When the flooding was over and the ark rested on top of Mount Ararat, God revealed another facet of His personality to Noah—ELOHIM, "the God Who makes covenants"! God first spoke as JEHOVAH and told Noah to make a sacrifice unto Him. The animals Noah offered made a sweet-smelling sacrifice to the Lord.

Then something beautiful happened:

> *And I will establish my covenant with you; neither shall all flesh be cut off any more by the waters of a flood; neither shall there any more be a flood to destroy the earth. And God said, This is the token of the covenant which I make between me and you and every living creature that is with you, for perpetual generations: I do set my bow in the cloud, and it shall be for a token of a covenant between me and the earth* (Genesis 9:11-13).

ELOHIM showed Himself in two ways: He created a rainbow by His mighty power, and He made a covenant with Noah. That rainbow was God's sign that told Noah, "I will never flood the earth again"; and the rainbow should still remind you and me of that same covenant. God, mighty and powerful, wants to protect His creation. When you see a rainbow, think of ELOHIM, the God Who enters into everlasting agreements with His people!

God made a covenant with Abraham also. The first time God ever spoke to Abraham (then, he was still called Abram) is recorded in Genesis 12:1-3. When God first spoke to him, He

14

used two names—JEHOVAH and ELOHIM:

> *Now the LORD had said unto Abram, Get thee out*
> *of thy country, and from thy kindred, and from thy*
> *father's house, unto a land that I will shew thee: And*
> *I will make of thee a great nation, and I will bless*
> *thee, and make thy name great; and thou shalt be a*
> *blessing: And I will bless them that bless thee, and*
> *curse him that curseth thee: and in thee shall all*
> *families of the earth be blessed.*

This is how God revealed Himself to Abraham—as a God of blessing! He was speaking as JEHOVAH. You will study the name JEHOVAH later, but these few verses will allow you to differentiate God as ELOHIM—the covenant God of might:

> *And Abraham said, Lord GOD, what wilt thou give*
> *me, seeing I go childless, and the steward of my*
> *house is this Eliezer of Damascus? And Abram said,*
> *Behold, to me thou hast given no seed: and, lo, one*
> *born in my house is mine heir.*
>
> *And, behold, the word of the LORD came unto him,*
> *saying, This shall not be thine heir; but he that shall*
> *come forth out of thine own bowels shall be thine*
> *heir. And he brought him forth abroad, and said,*
> *Look now toward heaven, and tell the stars, if thou*
> *be able to number them: and he said unto him, So*
> *shall thy seed be* (Genesis 15:2-5).

God was covenanting with Abram to give him a child. When

Abram said, "Lord, God," he was saying, "I know Your ways, because You have revealed them to me. But I want a covenant with You, because You are able to give me a child."

In this covenant God commanded Abram to do three things: (1) leave his country, (2) leave his relatives, and (3) travel to a land to which God would lead him. But Abram only obeyed two of the commands—although he left his country for the land of promise, he took his relatives with him.

Abram was accompanied by his nephew, **Lot**, meaning "a wrapping," and his father, **Terah**, meaning "delay." And Terah really created a delay for Abram. God wanted to make a covenant with Abram, who was to become the "father of faith," but Abram could not make the agreement while his eyes were on his family instead of on God.

While traveling to the land of promise, Terah, who was very old, needed to stop and rest. Abram, Lot, and Terah halted their journey at a place called **Haran**, which means "dry and parched." They stayed there until Terah died two years later. God had commanded Abram not to take his relatives, but because Abram did things his own way, he ended up in a dry, parched place where he couldn't hear from God.

We are supposed to love, honor, and obey our parents—that is a commandment from God Himself—but we are not to revere our relatives above the Word of God! That's when trouble comes. Let God have the very first place in your life. When you do, your spiritual walk will never become dry and parched; it will always be refreshing.

Abram had been delayed for almost two years; and when he finally did reach the Promised Land, he found famine. Imagine how discouraged he must have felt! After a two-year delay in this desert-land called Haran, Abram finally arrived at his destination only to find similarly terrible conditions. In addition, Abram hadn't heard from God in two years. Abram probably wondered whether he would ever hear God's voice again!

Many people wonder why God rarely speaks to them—when they haven't obeyed His first instruction. Silence may be God's way of saying, "You haven't finished what I asked you to complete. When you fully obey My first words, I'll speak to you again—but not until then!" It took Abram awhile to get the hint.

Now, in the land of promise, Abram built an altar between **Bethel**, which means "the house of God," and **Hai**, which means "a place of ruin." I would have built the temple right inside "the house of God," but Abram was just beginning to walk by faith. Perhaps he wasn't quite ready to build a temple in Bethel.

The major activity with which Abram concerned himself during his lifetime was building altars. He was a man who communed regularly with God (JEHOVAH). He highly esteemed the covenant God of might. One really positive point in Abram's story is that, although there were delays, God always overcame them.

Be encouraged by the accounts of those men of faith who paved our way. We have the opportunity to learn from their mistakes and to be encouraged by how God divinely overcame the flaws of their humanity.

Abram, his wife Sarai, and Lot traveled to Egypt to avoid the famine. When they returned Abram's altar had been destroyed, so he rebuilt it. Then Abram took his family and moved to a place between **Mamre**, which means "fatness," and **Hebron**, which means "fellowship." Perhaps this was Abram's way of saying, "Devil, you can't try to destroy what I've built! I'll just rebuild it. And not only that, but I'll build a second, even better altar."

Abram's new altar is significant, because it shows that his communion with God was flourishing. But Abram was still having trouble with unbelief concerning God's promise about his descendants. He and Sarai still had not had any children. Abram probably thought, "Just in case I don't receive children from God, I can raise my nephew Lot as my own child." Abram was trying to play it safe, just in case God didn't come through on His part of the bargain.

Eventually, however, Abram and Lot had no choice—they had to separate. And it turned out to be the best thing they did! They both had herdsmen who were tending flocks, and soon these herdsmen began to have great disagreements among themselves. One day, Abram confronted Lot:

> *And Abram said unto Lot, Let there be no strife, I*
> *pray thee, between me and thee, and between my*
> *herdmen and thy herdmen; for we be brethren. Is*
> *not the whole land before thee? separate thyself, I*
> *pray thee, from me: if thou wilt take the left hand,*
> *then I will go to the right; or if thou depart to the*
> *right hand, then I will go to the left* (Genesis 13:8-9).

Abram really exercised his godly qualities. He didn't say, "Well, Lot, since I'm older, you'd better honor me. I'll take the best portion of land." No! Abram said, "Lot, there are two sections of land: one to my right, and one to my left. You choose whichever you prefer, and I'll take the section that is left."

Many people who read this instantly think, "Abram was being humble; he didn't want to take the best for himself." But that was not true: Abram knew ELOHIM—"God Almighty" and "the

God Who made covenants." Abram didn't care which section of land Lot chose; because Abram knew that, regardless of where he lived, God would protect him.

Lot immediately looked around and saw two things:

> *And Lot lifted up his eyes, and beheld all the plain of Jordan, that it was well watered every where, before the* LORD *destroyed Sodom and Gomorrah, even as the garden of the* LORD, *like the land of Egypt, as thou comest unto Zoar* (Genesis 13:10).

Then Lot said, "Abram, I'll take that nice, well-watered plain over there. You can have the mountainous region." Having made their decisions, Lot and Abram separated. Abram and Sarai moved to the arid, mountainous area. And when they got there, what do you think happened? God spoke to Abraham again:

> *And the Lord said unto Abram, **after that Lot was separated from him,** Lift up now thine eyes, and look from the place where thou art northward, and southward, and eastward, and westward: For all the land which thou seest, to thee will I give it, and to thy seed for ever* (Genesis 13:14-15).

It must have been wonderful to hear from God again! And finally, Abram knew that the time was near to draw into a covenant with Almighty God. When God spoke this to Abram, he did not merely look around casually and say, "This, for me? Oh, God, how nice!" The Bible says that Abram lifted up his eyes! I believe he looked upward and received a vision—he saw what God saw—a vision of faith!

When Abram looked northward, I think he saw the entire northern part of the Holy Land. Southward, Abram saw far, far beyond the mountain that blocked his view. Eastward and westward, what do you think Abram saw? He probably saw all the way to the Mediterranean Sea and over into Jordan! Abram's relatives were out of the way—now he could focus his eyes on God, Who instructed him further:

> *"'Arise, walk through the land in the length of it and in the breadth of it; for I will give it unto thee'"* (Genesis 13:17).

A faith vision isn't enough. You have to do more than just have a vision—you have to live it! You must walk it!

I once heard about a man who would sit in his rocking chair on his front porch and say, "I wish I had a million dollars. I wish I had a million dollars." Do you think he ever received a million dollars? No! You can't obtain a million dollars while sitting in a rocking chair. You don't get things by wishing for them. Some people have the vision, but they don't have the action that goes with it and they miss out on their blessing.

God told Abram, "You have to act on this vision! Walk through the land; I will give you the land upon which you tread." I think Abram was the world's first jogger. He jogged north, south, east, and west.

I can imagine what the Canaanites said as Abram jogged past them: "Who is that man who just jogged down the road?"

"I don't know, but I saw him going the other way yesterday."

Abram was running as the man who would possess the land. He was thinking of God's promise that his seed's seed would possess the land! As he ran, I'm sure Abram said, "This is mine;

this is mine . . . ." as he prepared himself to enter into a covenant relationship with God.

But after Abram claimed that land, something happened—and it didn't surprise me a bit! A wicked king, named Chedorlaomer, roused a group of other kings; and they traveled down from Elam (present-day Iran) with trouble on their minds. They attacked Sodom and Gomorrah—land upon which Abram had trod—and abducted people and stole their possessions. The kings even captured Lot, Abram's nephew.

The devil will try to steal what you've claimed! When you claim something, and tread upon the ground of God's Word by speaking His promises, you had better prepare for battle. Some people stake their claims, but as soon as the enemy says, "You can't have that," they'll lie down and play dead! Of course the devil will try to steal your blessing—Jesus has told you that he would—but through Jesus you have power over Satan and can refuse to let him take anything from you.

Abram wasn't about to play the enemy's game—he really got bold. Abram said, "They can't do this! I trod upon this land, and it's mine. So I won't put up with the enemy's tricks."

I wondered, "How could one man be so bold?" But then I realized, **it's because he knew ELOHIM—the God of covenant relationships.** He knew God would not give him land if he couldn't keep it. That land was for his seed's seed. Abram banded together a group of men, and they went up to Elam and took back everything!

Some people say, "Nuclear weapons will destroy the world!" But that will never happen, because God is bigger, mightier, and more powerful than any bomb that man has ever made. God is not going to have His earth blown up until He is ready to finish it the way He wants. He will do it by fire, but I don't believe the fire will be started by an atomic bomb. I don't accept that, because God knows how to take care of His creation—and He has done so for a very long time.

God knows how to care for you, because you have entered into a covenant relationship with Him. By faith, you're the seed of Abraham; and God told Abraham, "Surely blessing I will bless you, and multiplying I will multiply you." He is your covenant-making God. He is the God of might and power. He strengthened Abram and gave him might and power to win, **and God will give you might and power to win also:**

> *In the same day the LORD made a covenant with Abram, saying, 'Unto thy seed have I given this land, from the river of Egypt unto the great river, the river Euphrates: The Kenites, and the Kenizzites, and the Kadmonites, And the Hittites, and the Perizzites, and the Rephaims, And the Amorites, and the Canaanites, and the Girgashites, and the Jebusites* (Genesis 15:18-21).

When He entered into a covenant with Abram, the Lord God said, "We have a relationship between ourselves, and I'm giving you all of this land."

What would it take for Abram and Sarai to realize the impact of having a covenant with Almighty God? At this point, all they seemed to realize was that they were supposed to have seed (children); and they still didn't have any! Abram must have thought, "It's going to take a lot of might and power to keep this covenant, because we're way past childbearing years!"

However, when Abram was 99 years old and Sarai was 89, God finally told them that they would have children. He also changed their names: Abram became **Abraham**, which means "father of a multitude," and Sarai became **Sarah**, which means "princess of many nations."

How could this be? The Bible says that Abraham laughed aloud when God changed his name—Abraham simply couldn't believe that he would father many nations! And Sarah laughed, too, when she overheard God telling Abraham that he would have a child. Abraham's divine Visitor said, "Sarah laughed"; and she was so embarrassed that she denied it.

However, Abraham and Sarah did have a child; and God prenamed the baby **Isaac**, which means "laughter." Abraham and Sarah both may have laughed, but God had the last laugh! Hebrews 11:11 talks about Isaac's birth: by faith Sarah received the strength to have that child. It took more than just Abraham's faith to have seed; both he and Sarah had to be in agreement! The word **strength** in Hebrew comes from the Greek word **dunamis**, meaning "miracle-working power." Who gave Sarah that miracle-working power? ELOHIM, the God of might and power!

You need to have a renewed image of the God of might and power—the God Who is more than able to put you over in any difficulty! If God (ELOHIM) is for you, who can possibly be against you? No one! ELOHIM is more powerful than any person or thing that exists, and He is on your side.

God wants you to rely on Him as your source of power and might. He wants to be ELOHIM **to** you, **for** you, and **in** you. Right now, no matter what the circumstances may be in your life, will you let Him renew your spirit, mind, body, emotions, and image? Everytime you see the word **God,** think, "That's ELOHIM, the God of might and power—and He's **my** God!" Praise the Lord!

Following are some scripture references that refer to God as ELOHIM. When you need His power and might to work in your life, read through these scriptures and refresh your vision of His covenant with you.

*I will say of the LORD, He is my refuge and my fortress: my God; in him will I trust. Surely he shall deliver thee from the snare of the fowler, and from the noisome pestilence. He shall cover thee with his feathers, and under his wings shalt thou trust; his truth shall be thy shield and buckler* (Psalm 91:2-4).

*And they shall be my people, and I will be their God: And I will give them one heart, and one way, that they may fear me for ever, for the good of them, and of their children after them: And I will make an everlasting covenant with them, that I will not turn away from them, to do them good; but I will put my fear in their hearts, that they shall not depart from me* (Jeremiah 32:38-40).

*And he* [Solomon] *said, LORD God of Israel, there is no God like thee, in heaven above, or on earth beneath, who keepest covenant and mercy with thy servants that walk before thee with all their heart* (I Kings 8:23).

*Be merciful unto me, O God, be merciful unto me: for my soul trusteth in thee: yea, in the shadow of thy wings will I make my refuge, until these calamities be overpast. I will cry unto God most high;*

*unto God that performeth all things for me. He shall send from heaven, and save me from the reproach of him that would swallow me up. Selah. God shall send forth his mercy and his truth* (Psalm 57:1-3).

# Chapter Two

# JEHOVAH

Derived from the Hebrew word **chavah**, which means "to live," the name JEHOVAH is literally full of life! It is written into the King James Version of the Bible as **LORD**, and it means "to be," or "being."

Now that you have seen God as the all-powerful, mighty ELOHIM, Who desires a covenant with those whom He created, you will love meeting Him as JEHOVAH—the revealing One! This name of God brings Him forth in a very personal way, and it is the very essence of the present tense.

When Adam and Eve talked to God in the garden of Eden, they did not call Him JEHOVAH; instead, they called Him ELOHIM, because they did not have a personal, intimate walk with the Lord.

Has the Lord ever spoken to you? He has spoken often to me through divine impression in my spirit. I have known that these sweet and precious messages were from the Lord—that is, JEHOVAH, the revealing One.

I remember a specific time when He characterized this wonderful side of His personality as I was praying. I said, "Lord, it's such a privilege to live for You."

And He said, "Marilyn, you don't live only **for** Me—you live **with** Me!"

JEHOVAH reveals Himself as your intimate, personal God. He walks with you—always in the present tense—and He will never leave nor forsake you. The more you grow in this relationship with Him, the more of Himself He will reveal to you.

JEHOVAH also denotes the unchangeability of God:

*"... with whom is no variableness, neither shadow of turning"* (James 1:17).

And Psalm 102:27 says *"But thou art the same, and thy years shall have no end."* JEHOVAH is the One Who is now, and always has been. This is the God of life, the God of eternity!

In our study of the name JEHOVAH, we will study the life of Moses in Exodus. Moses was called by God to deliver His people from Egypt. Moses' family was aware of his calling, and they were a family of faith. They were also enslaved to the Egyptian people. But through miraculous circumstances, Moses grew up in the Pharaoh's palace and was trained to be the next Pharaoh in line—quite a comfortable set of circumstances! To the natural eye, it probably appeared to Moses' parents that he couldn't possibly become a deliverer of the Hebrews. He had it made—why would he want to deliver the Israelites from the hand of the Egyptians?

But God will deal with someone until He wins! And God dealt with Moses. At 40 years of age, Moses finally decided that, since God had called him to deliver the Israelites, he may as well get on with it.

Did you ever try to help God? I know we all have at times, and Moses was no exception. His emotions overwhelmed him one day when he saw an Egyptian man beating one of the Israelites. Moses killed the Egyptian.

What a problem Moses' action created! The Egyptians were furious, and Moses had to flee for his life. Then the Egyptians really cracked down on the Israelites, which caused them to become enraged at Moses too!

Moses fled to a place called Midian, where he tended sheep for 40 years. I've often wondered about what he did during those 40 years. Some Bible scholars think he wrote the book of Job, and he very well could have. Some say he wrote Genesis, but I think Genesis was written on Mount Sinai along with the rest of the Pentateuch.

Moses gained wonderful experience on how to survive in the desert. And he would need this experience when he would lead the people out of Egypt into the Promised Land. Moses also learned about leading and caring for sheep—and people often resemble sheep. The prophet Isaiah said that we have all gone astray like sheep.

God is so economical! If you give Him the opportunity, He will use everything in your life to bring glory to His name. I'm sure Moses did not expect God to glorify his situation; in fact, I think Moses lost confidence that God would ever use him again. But Moses forgot that God plays until He wins. And when God wins, He wants to make you a winner too! Each victory is a credit to God! The apostle Paul said it well:

> *"Now thanks be unto God, which always causeth*
> *us to triumph in Christ, . . . "* (II Corinthians 2:14).

God set some high goals for Moses, because God wanted Moses to win.

God has set goals for all His people. Don't allow jealousy of other Christians to rule your life—you're a part of the same Body of Christ! Instead, support other Christians by saying, "When you're doing well, so am I; because we're a part of the same Body!

Whenever I visit Oral Roberts University, I don't get jealous. I don't complain, "God, why did You use Oral instead of me?" No! I let that stimulate my faith; and I say, "Dear God! If You can do it for Oral Roberts, I know You can do it for Marilyn Hickey too!"

Success is a credit to God's kingdom! Moses didn't have anyone around to stimulate his faith the way we can for each other, so God stepped into the scene with every intention of turning Moses into a winner—although Moses wasn't aware of it.

One day, Moses was tending sheep near a place called **Mount Horeb** (Sinai), which means "fresh inspiration." After 40 years in the wilderness, God was getting ready to give Moses fresh inspiration to accomplish His goal. God can give you fresh inspiration, even if you've really blown it! He will always pick you up; He will never put you down!

Moses was minding his own business when, suddenly, he noticed a burning bush. This was not an ordinary bush, however—the fire never consumed the bush! Then God spoke to Moses from the fire:

> *... God called unto him out of the midst of the bush, and said, Moses, Moses. and he said, Here am I. And he said, Draw not nigh hither: put off thy shoes from off thy feet, for the place whereon thou standest is holy ground* (Exodus 3:4-5).

What a shock! I don't think Moses had ever expected to hear the Lord again:

> *And the LORD said, I have surely seen the affliction of my people which are in Egypt, and have heard their cry by reason of their taskmasters; for I know their sorrows; And I am come down to deliver them out of the hand of the Egyptians, and to bring them up out of that land unto a good land and a large, unto a land flowing with milk and honey; unto the place of the Canaanites, and the Hittites, and the Amorites, and the Perizzites, and the Hivites, and the Jebusites* (Exodus 3:7-8).

Basically, God was saying, "Moses, you're still the man I want to use to deliver My people."

Moses was 80 years old now, and I'm sure he was quite surprised to learn that he was going to lead the Israelites out of Egypt. Forty years earlier he may have said, "Don't you know that I am your deliverer?" Now he was saying, "Who am I? I've blown it so badly I couldn't deliver anything!"

But God was saying, "You're ready to be a deliverer."

God specializes in creating winners! He said, "I will be with you and give you a token of My presence, Moses. You will go back and lead My people out of Egypt; and then you'll return to this mountain and serve Me."

Mount Horeb was where God gave Moses the Ten Commandments and where Moses spent precious time with JEHOVAH, the revealing One! Moses said, "The children of Israel will ask me Your Name—and I don't even know it!"

God replied, "You just tell them that I AM sent you."

Who is "I AM"? He's JEHOVAH, the One Who revealed Himself to the children of Israel! Not only did He reveal Himself to them, but He also revealed His plan to deliver them from the Egyptians and lead them into the Promised Land. God didn't want Moses to limit Him with one name; instead, God planned to be all that the children of Israel would need:

> *"And God said unto Moses, 'I AM THAT I AM:' and he said, 'Thus shalt thou say unto the children of Israel, I AM hath sent me unto you' "* (Exodus 3:14).

God revealed Himself as JEHOVAH—the One Who is the same yesterday, today, and forever! He was saying, "I am Abraham's God, Isaac's God, Jacob's God, and I am YOUR God!

Generations change, but I will never change."

God showed that Moses was to be the person who would deliver the Israelites from the hand of the Egyptians. Although God may have been full of plans, Moses was full of excuses.

Moses said, "The elders of Israel aren't going to buy this, God. After all, look at what happened the last time."

God asked, "What's that in your hand?"

"It's a rod, Lord."

"Throw it down on the ground."

Then Moses cast the rod to the ground, and the rod became a serpent. Moses tried to run away; but God said, "Pick it up, Moses."

Moses picked up the serpent and, immediately, it became a rod again! Although God told Moses, "I will give that sign to the elders and to Pharaoh," Moses was still skeptical. He just couldn't imagine himself as much of a deliverer. Then God said, "If that isn't enough, Moses, I'll give you another sign."

> *And the LORD said furthermore unto him, Put now thine hand into thy bosom. And he put his hand into his bosom: and when he took it out, behold, his hand was leprous as snow. And he said, Put thine hand into thy bosom again. And he put his hand into his bosom again; and plucked it out of his bosom, and, behold, it was turned again as his other flesh* (Exodus 4:6-7).

Moses' leprous hand signified that Moses was led by the wrong motive to deliver when he killed the Egyptian man. Moses was trying to deliver by himself and was not following JEHOVAH. God had not yet revealed Himself to Moses.

However, when Moses put his hand on his heart a second time, his hand became clean. This signified that Moses was now led by the correct motive to deliver the Israelites. This time, when Moses went forth to deliver, signs would accompany his calling.

God silenced all Moses' arguments. Moses was still holding out, though. He said, "Lord, I just can't do it. I don't speak well enough."

At this point the Lord must have thought, "That's not even true"; because Acts 7:22 says that Moses was "mighty in word and deed." Moses had received the finest Egyptian training and had been educated to be an eloquent public speaker. Perhaps his exile in the desert had given him a poor self-image; however, God had heard enough excuses:

> *And the LORD said unto him, Who hath made man's mouth? or who maketh the dumb, or deaf, or the seeing, or the blind? have not I the LORD? Now therefore go, and I will be with thy mouth, and teach thee what thou shalt say* (Exodus 4:11-12).

What an excellent reply! JEHOVAH had to remind Moses that He is also the powerful Creator, ELOHIM; and He told Moses, "Look! If you're going to drag around, we'll get Aaron, your brother, to speak for you. Besides, all the men who sought your life are dead; so you don't have to worry about a thing."

This retort stripped away Moses' last excuse. He probably thought that he'd be facing people who wanted his head, but JEHOVAH convinced Moses to lead the people. As it turned out, Aaron never did any of the speaking. Moses did all of it. After all, when the Lord God is on your side, who else do you need?

When Moses arrived in Egypt, God gave demonstrations of His power as ELOHIM. As Moses spoke the Word, and God was revealed as JEHOVAH—"I AM," mighty works followed. Every plague upon the Egyptians was a judgment against an idol they worshiped. They worshiped the Nile river, and it was turned into blood. They worshiped a frog god called "Heki" and mummified frogs; so God said, "You like frogs? I'll give you lots of them!"

The Egyptians also worshiped a sun god called "Ra," so God plagued them with a very discriminating darkness that covered only their homes. Light continued to shine in Goshen, where the Israelites lived.

I'm sure that the Pharaoh was suspicious of this supernatural event. God was trying to win the Egyptians, as well as the Israelites—He loves the sinner too! Through these mighty signs God was saying, "Your idols are wrong. Turn to Me."

Finally, the Pharaoh released the children of Israel. I think a lot of the Egyptians were won over, also, because the Bible says that "a mixed multitude" followed Moses out of Egypt into the wilderness.

But the trials weren't over yet. God really took care of those people. Their shoes and garments didn't wear out, and they even had heating and air conditioning. A cloud cover by day and a pillar of fire by night shielded them from scorching days and bitterly cold desert nights. God even acted as their military protection. Who else would part a body of water so that they could pass through without being harmed?

But how easily they seemed to forget about the miracle-working God Who loved and protected them. The children of Israel started to murmur, and that didn't go over well with either God nor Moses.

Exodus 31 describes many of the Israelites' experiences as they sojourned through the wilderness and arrived at Mount Horeb, where Moses had first heard God's voice from the burning bush.

God took Moses to the mountaintop and gave him the Ten Commandments. I also believe this is where God revealed Genesis to Moses. Moses wasn't just sitting idly up on the mountain for 40 days, although a lot of people probably imagine that. I'm sure God kept Moses busy.

While Moses was up on Mount Horeb, things weren't going at all well with the Israelites. They didn't expect Moses to be gone this long. Maybe they thought he could just say, "Well, Lord, this is taking quite a while, and it's getting late. I have to get back to my people."

It doesn't work that way. The people really got restless, and finally, they rebelled:

> *And when the people saw that Moses delayed to come down out of the mount, the people gathered themselves together unto Aaron, and said unto him, Up, make us gods, which shall go before us; for as for this Moses, the man that brought us up out of the land of Egypt, we wot not what is become of him* (Exodus 32:1).

When God heard about what was going on with the people, He really got angry. He said, "Moses, get down there! I'm disgusted with those people!"

And in His righteous indignation, God was revealing Himself as JEHOVAH. The Lord's personality is that of pure righteousness and holiness. Consider Leviticus 19:2, which says,

*" . . . Ye shall be holy: for I the LORD your God am holy."*
Translated, this actually means, "I JEHOVAH your ELOHIM
am holy." It is Jehovah Who must pronounce the judgment
that condemns sin . . . and He was really ready to pronounce
judgment against the children of Israel for worshiping the gods
of Egypt!

God said, "Moses, you go tell your people that you brought
out of Egypt that I will wipe them out! We'll start over again,
and I'll make you into a great nation."

Wait a minute! Are those really Moses' people? In
Exodus 3:7, JEHOVAH had told Moses, " . . . I have surely
seen the affliction of my people . . . ":

> *Now therefore let me alone, that my wrath may wax*
> *hot against them, and that I may consume them:*
> *and I will make of thee a great nation. And Moses*
> *besought the LORD his God, and said, LORD, why*
> *doth thy wrath wax hot against thy people, which*
> *thou has brought forth out of the land of Egypt*
> *with great power, and with a mighty hand?*
> (Exodus 32:10-11).

Moses had been walking with JEHOVAH for perhaps a year.
He said, "God, You're the One Who brought these people forth
as their ELOHIM of power! And they're not my people—they're
Yours!"

No one would talk to the Lord like that unless he or she
knew Him really well. Moses was actually arguing with God,
Who had already said, "That's My decision. Now leave Me
alone!"

Then Moses said something really interesting:

> *Wherefore should the Egyptians speak, and say, For
> mischief did he bring them out, to slay them in the
> mountains, and to consume them from the face of
> the earth? Turn from thy fierce wrath, and repent
> of this evil against thy people* (Exodus 32:12).

What an appeal! I can just see Moses telling JEHOVAH, "If
You kill those people, You are really going to hurt Your
reputation, God. The Egyptians are going to say, 'Look at that
God! He's not so hot. He brought those people out into the
desert and got mad at them, just like He did to us, and wiped
them out!' God, if You wipe them out, Your reputation will be
hurt."

Moses was appealing to "the revealing One." But Moses wasn't
quite finished:

> *Remember Abraham, Isaac, and Israel, thy servants,
> to whom thou swarest by thine own self, and saidst
> unto them, I will multiply your seed as the stars of
> heaven, and all this land that I have spoken of will
> I give unto your seed, and they shall inherit it for
> ever* (Exodus 32:13).

Moses prayed God's Word: "God, what about Your promise
to Abraham, Isaac, and Jacob? You said You'd make of their
seed a great nation—You won't be honoring Your Word."
And what do you think Jehovah did?

> *"And the LORD repented of the evil which he
> thought to do unto his people"* (Exodus 32:14).

JEHOVAH took the people back as His own. Why? Because

Moses prayed the Word, and God says that He magnifies His Word above His name.

Moses went down the mountain with the tablets containing God's commandments. And when he neared the bottom, he discovered why the Lord had been so angry. There was noise, commotion, people dancing . . . and there sat a golden calf being worshiped.

Moses got angry! He was furious at their sin, probably from spending so much time with JEHOVAH God, Who loves sinners, but hates sin:

> *Then Moses stood in the gate of the camp, and said, Who is on the LORD'S side? let him come unto me. And all the sons of Levi gathered themselves together unto him* (Exodus 32:26).

All of Moses' immediate family from the tribe of Levi came and stood with Moses:

> *And he said unto them, Thus saith the LORD God of Israel, Put every man his sword by his side, and go in and out from gate to gate throughout the camp, and slay every man his brother, and every man his companion, and every man his neighbour. And the children of Levi did according to the word of Moses: and there fell of the people that day about three thousand men* (Exodus 32:27,28).

Moses' successful intercession with God to accept the people didn't mean everything was a bed of roses again. Sin is still sin. Moses gave **all** of the people an opportunity to repent.

He argued with God for the people. Then Moses went to the people and told them to stop sinning.

Those who hardened their hearts were put to death. You might think, "They had it tough. No one gets put to death for sinning anymore." Oh no? Romans 8:6 says to be carnally minded is "death"; but to be spiritually minded is "life and peace."

Moses gave all the people a chance to choose life, but only the sons of Levi made the right decision. After the unrighteous died in battle, Moses went before JEHOVAH again and took a priestly stand:

> *And Moses returned to the LORD, and said, Oh, this people have sinned a great sin, and have made them gods of gold. Yet now, if thou wilt forgive their sin—; and if not, blot me, I pray thee, out of thy book which thou has written* (Exodus 32:31-32).

Do you want others to win, or do you just want to win yourself? If you really want to have a heart that flows with God's will, have a heart like Moses. He had favor with God, but he used that favor to save his nation. Moses entered into his calling as a priest, and in doing so, he entered into the personality of JEHOVAH Himself:

> *And the LORD said unto Moses, Whosoever hath sinned against me, him will I blot out of my book. Therefore now go, lead the people unto the place of which I have spoken unto thee: behold, mine Angel shall go before thee: nevertheless in the day when I visit I will visit their sin upon them. And the LORD plagued the people, because they made the calf, which Aaron made* (Exodus 32:33-35).

God still dealt with the people for their sin. Some people will say, "I've repented, so everything is all right." That is "greasy grace and sloppy agape." There is still a law that began in the very beginning of Genesis, and it is the law of sowing and reaping. Some Christians want to make up their own rules as they go—but they cannot bend that law:

> *And the LORD said unto Moses, Depart, and go up hence, thou and the people which thou hast brought up out of the land of Egypt, unto the land which I sware unto Abraham, to Isaac, and to Jacob, saying, Unto thy seed will I give it: And I will send an angel before thee; . . . for I will not go up in the midst of thee; for thou art a stiffnecked people: lest I consume thee in the way* (Exodus 33:1-3).

God told these people, "I'll send an angel before you to bring you into the Promised Land—but I'm not going, because I cannot stand your rebellion." Then the people took off all their heathen ornaments and stood in the doorways of their tents. Moses went to the tabernacle and entered his priestly role again to commune with God.

When he got there, the cloud descended upon the tabernacle—and the children of Israel must have thought, "What a relief!"

> *And all the people saw the cloudy pillar stand at the tabernacle door: and all the people rose up and worshiped, every man in his tent door. And the LORD spake unto Moses face to face, as a man speaketh unto his friend. And he turned again into*

41

> *the camp: but his servant Joshua, the son of Nun,*
> *a young man, departed not out of the tabernacle.*
>
> *And Moses said unto the LORD, See, thou sayest*
> *unto me, Bring up this people: and thou hast not*
> *let me know whom thou wilt send with me. Yet thou*
> *hast said, I know thee by name, and thou hast also*
> *found grace in my sight* (Exodus 33:10-12).

Moses was after God again! He was saying. "God, You haven't said which angel is going to take us into the Promised Land. Remember, God, You called me by name and gave me grace and favor in Your sight—and if You won't go with us and consider this nation as Your people, we're not going at all!"

Moses could have said, "I've had it with that crowd and their murmuring!" But he didn't.

How could he talk with God in this way? Because he knew God as JEHOVAH! Moses had an intimate relationship with his Lord.

And what did God say to him?

> *"And he said, 'My presence shall go with thee, and*
> *I will give thee rest.' And he said unto him, 'If thy*
> *presence go not with me, carry us not up hence'"*
> (Exodus 33:14-15).

God went with them. The presence of the Lord was promised by God, and His presence finally brought the people into rest. But Moses wasn't finished with God. Moses said, "Lord, I beseech You, show me Your glory."

Moses was a spiritual opportunist, and God liked that quality.

God doesn't have pets. Some Christians get more because they stick with it and ask for more! God didn't turn Moses down when he became bold. God said this to Moses:

> *And he said, I will make all my goodness pass before thee, and I will proclaim the name of the LORD before thee; and will be gracious to whom I will be gracious, and will shew mercy on whom I will shew mercy. And he said, Thou canst not see my face: for there shall no man see me, and live.*
>
> *And the LORD said, Behold, there is a place by me, and thou shalt stand upon a rock: And it shall come to pass, while my glory passeth by, that I will put thee in a clift of the rock, and will cover thee with my hand while I pass by: And I will take away mine hand, and thou shalt see my back parts: but my face shall not be seen* (Exodus 33:19-23).

Moses got what he asked for, didn't he? Why? Because he said, "I want to see Your glory—I desire an even closer relationship with You, JEHOVAH!"

God has wonderful things in store for those who desire the closeness with Him that Moses had. When I read this, I want to weep, because I really see what the Lord has done for you and me: He has called us to enter our priesthood.

JEHOVAH did not call us to condemn us—He called us to be reconciled with Him. He called us to reconcile the world to Him and to make the world winners! JEHOVAH has called us to go before God in prayer and intercession: "God, have mercy upon them! God, save them!"

What about our priestly calling toward the world? "Get saved! Get right with God, and get the sin out of your life!" Why? Because we want people to win. We want them to have life, and we want them to have it more abundantly.

When you take on the priestly calling of JEHOVAH (the Lord Who lives in you), He will reveal Himself through you to others.

JEHOVAH is a beautiful name—the ever-revealing One. Zechariah prophesied, saying, in the day of redemption, we shall see JEHOVAH. He prophesied to the nation of Israel, saying, "You are going to look on Him Whom you have pierced."

Who was he talking about? Jesus! If you study JEHOVAH from one end of the Bible to the other, you will find that He is the Lord Jesus Christ: JEHOVAH, revealed to you!

If you need a special revelation of Who God is, read through these scriptures which show Him as LORD. Let Him, the personal, ever-revealing One in your life, fill you with the revelation of His redeeming mercy:

> *"But the mercy of the LORD is from everlasting to everlasting upon them that fear him, and his righteousness unto children's children"*
> (Psalm 103:17).

> *Tell ye, and bring them near; yea, let them take counsel together: who hath declared this from ancient time? who hath told it from that time? have not I the LORD? and there is no God else beside me; a just God and a Saviour; there is none beside me*
> (Isaiah 45:21).

> *And I will bring the third part through the fire, and*

44

---

*will refine them as silver is refined, and will try them as gold is tried: they shall call on my name, and I will hear them: I will say, It is my people: and they shall say, The LORD is my God* (Zechariah 13:9).

*The fear of the LORD is the beginning of knowledge: but fools despise wisdom and instruction. My son, hear the instruction of thy father, and forsake not the law of thy mother: For they shall be an ornament of grace unto thy head, and chains about thy neck* (Proverbs 1:7-9).

*O LORD, thou hast searched me, and known me. Thou knowest my downsitting and mine uprising, thou understandest my thought afar off. Thou compassest my path and my lying down, and art acquainted with all my ways. For there is not a word in my tongue, but, lo, O LORD, thou knowest it altogether. Thou hast beset me behind and before, and laid thine hand upon me* (Psalm 139:1-5).

# Chapter Three

# EL SHADDAI

When you first studied the name ELOHIM, you discovered that EL displays God's qualities of power and might. EL SHADDAI is also a compound name that first appears in Genesis 17:

> *And when Abram was ninety years old and nine, the LORD appeared to Abram, and said unto him, I am the Almighty God; walk before me, and be thou perfect. And I will make my covenant between me and thee, and will multiply thee exceedingly* (Genesis 17:1-2).

Does "God Almighty" mean the same as "the God of might and power"? No, it does not. The name EL SHADDAI bears a different meaning entirely. Basically, this name is derived from the word "field," as the fields produce abundance. It is also translated as "breast," or "the many breasted One," which signifies nourishment and productiveness. In this sense, God is shown as the One Who is more than enough—He Who is all sufficient! When you see the name EL SHADDAI, God is saying, "I am more than enough to meet your needs in each situation."

Throughout Abraham's life, God promised to bless and multiply him. And the Bible says that Abraham's blessings are also ours. As EL SHADDAI, God came to Abraham in the context of total impossibility. He came saying, "I'll give you seed as the dust of the earth," when Abraham was 99 years old. And if that's not "impossible" enough, Abraham's wife was 89 years old. God shows His all sufficiency by turning nature around and providing a miracle that is contrary to natural events. Although God Himself set the course of nature in motion, He

48

is more than capable of superceding all natural events! That's what happened when He caused Abraham and Sarah to have a child.

Abraham's son was named Isaac, and Isaac also knew God as EL SHADDAI. When Isaac's own son Jacob left home to find a wife, Isaac spoke to him:

*And Isaac called Jacob, and blessed him, and charged him, and said unto him, Thou shalt not take a wife of the daughters of Canaan. Arise, go to Padan-aram, to the house of Bethuel thy mother's father; and take thee a wife from thence of the daughters of Laban thy mother's brother. And God Almighty bless thee, and make thee fruitful, and multiply thee, that thou mayest be a multitude of people* (Genesis 28:1-3).

Isaac was saying, "Jacob, may EL SHADDAI, the God Who is all sufficient, bless you and multiply you! He will work contrary to nature to overcome any difficult curcumstances."

Jacob left home with his father's blessings and the birthright—but with nothing in his hand. In fact, he left behind an irate brother, whom he had cheated out of the birthright. The brother's name was Esau, and he was more than ready to kill Jacob. Jacob had been a "mother's boy," and he was entering a totally strange situation that didn't look prosperous at all!

On the way to Padan-aram, Jacob slept and dreamed of a ladder on which angels ascended and descended. God spoke to him, "I'm giving this land to you and your seed, and I am going to protect you."

Greatly encouraged, Jacob continued on his way. When he arrived, he fell in love with a beautiful girl named Rachel. But Rachel's father Laban didn't possess many beautiful qualities; he was tricky and mean. He told Jacob that he could work seven years to pay for Rachel—but Laban gave Jacob Leah, Rachel's older sister, instead. Then Jacob had to work another seven years in order to have Rachel as his wife too.

To top all of this off, Laban changed Jacob's wages ten times, and Laban kept stealing Jacob's things. Jacob was in a horrible predicament. Finally, God spoke to him and said, "I want you to return to the Promised Land."

Jacob may have thought, "Well, I'll go back poor, but anything is better than living with Laban." But the God Who is more than enough intended to prosper him.

Some people want everything right away: instant coffee, instant tea, instant answer to prayer. But there's more to it than instant everything. You have to hold fast to your confidence in order to obtain rewards. You have to be patient and know that God is never late. Sometimes He's just in time, but He is never late. Last minute or not, hold fast to Him the way Jacob did and you won't miss the recompense of your reward.

God told Jacob, "I will bless and prosper you, if you will follow these instructions: when the cattle are taking water, where they usually mate, place speckled, spotted and striped stakes in the ground; let them watch the stakes, and you keep your eyes on them too. Then, when they conceive, they will have speckled, spotted, and striped animals. Those animals will be yours."

Jacob told Laban, "For my hire, when I leave, I want to take with me all of the speckled, spotted, and striped animals that are born."

Laban thought, "Great! There are hardly ever any of those."

He told Jacob, "That's just fine." Laban really regretted it later, because all of the babies born that year were spotted, speckled, and striped!

Jacob and his animals kept seeing those stakes. God set forth a vision to bring His Word to pass, and Jacob left as a very wealthy man. Why? Because the all-sufficient EL SHADDAI was in control. EL SHADDAI took hold of the natural things and turned them around into supernatural miracles. Jacob knew EL SHADDAI, as did his father Isaac and his grandfather Abraham.

Genesis 35 tells of a third vision that Jacob had:

> *And God appeared unto Jacob again, when he came out of Padan-aram, and blessed him. And God said unto him, Thy name is Jacob: thy name shall not be called any more Jacob, but Israel shall be thy name: and he called his name Israel. And God said unto him, I am God Almighty: be fruitful and multiply; a nation and a company of nations shall be of thee, and kings shall come out of thy loins* (Genesis 35:9-11).

Jacob had lived in the midst of strange circumstances and strange people; but God said, "Your situation doesn't matter! I am what matters. Let Me turn your circumstances around and bless you!"

God brought Jacob out from Laban's household as a wealthy man, reconciled him with his once-angry brother Esau, and gave him many children. Jacob lived as a wealthy, blessed man of a ripe, old age, because he knew EL SHADDAI.

The word "almighty" always relates to blessings and

multiplication. Because that name speaks of **more** than enough, it speaks of abundances. When Jesus said, "I came to give you life and give it to you more abundantly," He was speaking of EL SHADDAI, Who supplies abundances of nourishment for body, soul, and spirit.

Moses also knew EL SHADDAI. God spoke to him this way in Exodus 6:

> *And I appeared unto Abraham, unto Isaac, and*
> *unto Jacob, by the name of God Almighty, but*
> *by my name JEHOVAH was I not known to them*
> (Exodus 6:3).

God was saying, "I appeared to them as the God Who is more than enough, and I'm speaking to you too."

Then Moses wrote this in Psalm 91:

> *"He that dwelleth in the secret place of the most*
> *High shall abide under the shadow of the Almighty"*
> (Psalm 91:1).

Then Moses extols the power of God, which delivered them from the plagues that were upon Egypt. In this verse, the word **dwelleth** actually means "to stake your claim." Imagine this: he that stakes his claim in the secret place of the most High shall abide under the shadow of the Almighty. Moses said, "I'm staking my claim under the shadow of God Who is more than enough. That's where I want to live."

I want to live there too!

When Moses staked that claim, he really saw results! He was saying, "My God is more than enough to feed two million people. My God is all sufficient. And even though we're in the wilderness, these two million people will have water. No matter how tough my circumstances may appear, I'm counting on EL SHADDAI to bring us through!"

And He always did bring them through. That is why Hebrews 11 says that Moses forsook the pleasures of living in the Pharaoh's house and sojourned in the wilderness with the children of Israel. He stretched his faith out there and said, "I don't need the comforts of Pharaoh's house—my Almighty God has all that I need!"

Throughout his walk with the Lord, Moses kept on seeing the miraculous hand of God overcome nature itself. For 40 years, those people had no grocery bill, no water bill, no heating or air conditioning bills, and they never had to buy new shoes nor garments.

That is just tremendous—and if God could do it back then for two million people, don't you think He will take care of you now? Stake your claim under the shadow of EL SHADDAI. He's more than enough—more than you will ever need!

Do you want to dwell in the secret place of the Most High? Do you want to abide under the shadow of the Almighty?

*"I will say of the LORD, He is my refuge and my fortress: my God; in him will I trust"* (Psalm 91:2).

Stake your claim with your mouth. Moses did that, and you should too. Begin saying what you need God to be in your situation: "He's more than enough to heal me. He's more than enough to meet my financial needs. He's more than enough to get my children to repent. He's more than enough to put my marriage back together." Live under the shadow of the knowledge of a God Who is more than enough. He will turn the natural things around so that you will come through completely whole and completely blessed!

Have you ever heard of "claim jumpers"? In Colorado there are people who stake a claim on land that belongs to someone else. Sometimes they even remove another person's stakes and put theirs up instead.

The devil is a claim jumper, and he'll try to steal what you have claimed. But the Bible says He Who promised is faithful, and you have to push the devil right back off your claim! If you move out and don't hang onto your claim, you'll miss it. If you have already moved out, repent and get back in there! Put your trust in the all-sufficient One.

Joseph is another man who knew EL SHADDAI. He was Jacob's son, and Jacob prophesied something wonderful over him:

> *Joseph is a fruitful bough, even a fruitful bough by a well; whose branches run over the wall: The archers have sorely grieved him, and shot at him, and hated him: But his bow abode in strength, and the arms of his hands were made strong by the hands of the mighty God of Jacob; (from thence is the shepherd, the stone of Israel:)*

> *Even by the God of thy father, who shall help thee; and by the Almighty, who shall bless thee with blessings of heaven above, blessings of the deep that lieth under, blessings of the breasts, and of the womb: The blessings of thy father have prevailed above the blessings of my progenitors unto the utmost bound*

*of the everlasting hills: they shall be on the head
of Joseph, and on the crown of the head of him that
was separate from his brethren* (Genesis 49:22-26).

Jacob was saying, "Joseph, EL SHADDAI will bless you
abundantly and powerfully with all kinds of prosperity. You will
be prospered in every direction that you take, because He is
the God of abundance."

Fathers passed the blessings of Almighty God on to their
children, because God's promises were to their seed's seed.
Notice that Jacob didn't just assume that, because God had
said it, his seed would be blessed. He agreed with God and
spoke it out loud.

Did it come to pass? Yes. Jacob shared one of his visions
with Joseph in Genesis 48:

*And Jacob said unto Joseph, God Almighty appeared
unto me at Luz in the land of Canaan, and blessed
me, And said unto me, Behold, I will make thee
fruitful, and multiply thee, and I will make of thee
a multitude of people; and will give this land to thy
seed after thee for an everlasting possession*
(Genesis 48:3-4).

How could Jacob make all of those bold statements? Because
he knew EL SHADDAI, and he had his eyes under the shadow
of God Who is more than enough.

The Bible says that Abraham's blessings rest upon us. And
those blessings are from EL SHADDAI. That's Jesus saying
to you, "I came to give you life in abundance!" He never said
that He came just to squeeze you down into a nub and to get

you into heaven by the skin of your teeth. No, He has an abundance of God's blessings that are just for you. You need to camp with your mouth under God's shadow, and allow Him to be more than enough.

In the book of Numbers, just before the Israelites went forth to take the land of promise, something happened that really ruined it for them. The men went into the land and looked around to see what they would be claiming. When they came back, they said, "The land is beautiful, but there are giants in there. We'll never take the land." Those men brought back an evil report—it was a report that did not agree with the Word of God!

What happened? God said, "Because you would not let me be EL SHADDAI—more than enough to put you over—you're not going in! Only your children will go in."

Moses' three major sermons are found in the book of Deuteronomy. He was preaching God's Word to the young men who were supposed to enter and take the Promised Land. Why? It's the Word of God that gives people enough faith to take that land! Faith cometh by hearing and hearing by the Word of God. He knew, in order to take the Promised Land, they would have to be mighty men of faith.

When they finally took the land, it was by faith. By that time, Moses had died, and they had to capture a city called Jericho. God gave them a unique battle plan: He told the men to march around the city daily for six days and seven times on the seventh day.

After they marched around it the last time, he had them shout, and the walls came crashing down! Where did the faith come from? From the preaching of Moses, who told them about God Almighty-EL SHADDAI. He had said, "Place your trust in EL SHADDAI. He will turn natural circumstances around and give you supernatural miracles!"

EL SHADDAI—He is the **mighty One** Who can overrule natural events. The book of Numbers tells a story about a man named Balaam, who found out about God's overruling power. Balaam was a man of God, but Balaam had a bad background—he had once been a wizard.

Balaam used to prophesy evil and put curses on people— just like his father—but then Balaam got turned around and turned on to God.

During Balaam's life, there was trouble between the Israelites and the people of Moab. The Moabite king was really afraid of the Israelites, because he thought they might start a battle. God had warned the children of Israel to leave the Moabites alone, but this king was still fearful.

Finally, the king thought, "If we can put a curse on them, they'll never defeat us in battle." That king didn't realize with Whom he was dealing! It was foolish of him to think that he could defeat the Israelites through occult power.

The king sent for Balaam and said, "Curse those Israelites, and I'll pay you a lot of money." The king didn't know that Balaam had become a man of God. Balaam went to the Lord and asked, "What should I do?"

The Lord said, "Don't you dare curse My people! You know better than that, because no one can curse what I have blessed!" That was God's direction to Balaam. After Balaam refused, the Moabites offered him more money.

The devil came to tempt Jesus three times—Satan will **always** come back, and you need to make up your mind to stand against his tactics! Balaam could have stood against those men with the Word of God, but he didn't. Instead, his old nature began to rise up. He was tempted.

He did go before the Lord again, but God had already told him not to curse the Israelites! Now the Lord said, "Balaam, don't you do anything until they call for you in the morning."

The more Balaam considered that money, the further God's Word slipped from Balaam's mind. However, instead of heeding God's advice, Balaam thought, "I'm not going to wait around until morning!" And he left on his way to accept the king of Moab's offer.

But look what happened! His donkey crushed his foot against a stone wall and an angel blocked his way. God was really trying to change Balaam's mind about cursing the Israelites, but He will never force anyone to do anything.

God's directive will is in His Word. You can break it and go around it if you desire to, and He won't kill you. But when you're outside of God's will, you're in Satan's territory. And that's exactly where Balaam was treading.

When Balaam arrived at Moab, the king brought him to a mountaintop and said, "There are the Israelites that I want you to curse." So Balaam started calling for enchantments—trying to bring up demonic spirits—but they wouldn't come. Instead, you'll be amazed at what happened:

*"He hath said, which heard the words of God, which saw the vision of the Almighty, falling into a trance, but having his eyes open"* (Numbers 24:4).

God put a vision on Balaam. EL SHADDAI stepped in and gave Balaam a supernatural vision that opened his spiritual eyes. There was the Moabite king, waiting to hear Balaam curse the Israelites. Balaam said:

*How goodly are thy tents, O Jacob, and thy*

*tabernacles, O Israel! As the valleys are they spread forth, as gardens by the river's side, as the trees of lign aloes which the LORD hath planted, and as cedar trees beside the waters* (Numbers 24:5-6).

Balaam just went on and on with wonderful words like that. He even prophesied Jacob's star, which would lead the wise men to Jesus! Balaam prophesied that *"God is not a man that He should lie."*

What made Balaam say all of those good things? God's overruling will! When Balaam tried to bring forth seducing spirits, God just gave him a vision; and all Balaam could speak was the wonderful Word of God!

How could God do this? He is EL SHADDAI, the God Who is more than enough! He is so wonderful that someone tried to curse His people, and He turned that curse into a blessing!

Balak tried three times, on three different mountains, to get Balaam to curse the Israelites, and all Balaam could do was prophesy good things over them.

Finally, Balak said, "You're not doing it at all!"

EL SHADDAI will work contrary to every natural circumstance, so that **He can be the One Who is all sufficient!**

Job also knew EL SHADDAI. The name EL SHADDAI is used 48 times in the Bible, and 30 of those times are in the book of Job! Job doesn't seem like a book where God would show Himself as more than enough, but EL SHADDAI can work around total disaster!

When there seemed to be no way out for Job, Almighty God came on the scene and did some of His greatest miracles.

Job lost everything! He lost his children, health, possessions, and money. It really looked like he was "down the tubes." In fact, at one point he really would have seemed to be better off dead.

There was Job, lonely, poor, wretched, and miserable, when along came a "friend" named Eliphaz who said, "Job! You must have really done something wrong! What did you do to deserve this punishment from God?"

Job had enough trouble without Eliphaz adding to his problems. But Job kept saying, **"God is more than enough."** Job staked his claim under the shadow of Almighty God:

> *"Let us hold fast the profession of our faith without wavering; . . . "* (Hebrews 10:23).

That is exactly what Job did! Galatians 6:9 says that you will reap in due season—if you don't faint!

Job almost fainted—but he had staked a claim, and although he was bent, he didn't break! At the end of the book, God came on the scene and gave Job a double portion of the blessings he had before.

James 5:11 says that you should consider the end of Job. I've heard lots of people spend quite a bit of time considering the beginning of Job, but that's not what God's Word emphasized! God is saying, "Hang in there! Let Me bless you!"

Job ended up with ten more children. He lived about 70 more years. He was tremendously wealthy. His latter years were far more blessed than his former years. But he had to hang on for nine months—and he did it.

How? He knew EL SHADDAI. I can hear Job saying, **"He's more than enough! My God is more than enough!"** Job didn't faint, and he reaped his reward.

In the book of Ruth, there is a rather sad story about a woman named Naomi. She moved with her family from Bethlehem into Moab, which was a cursed place. She shouldn't have moved there, but there was a famine in Bethlehem. She didn't know that God was all sufficient to feed her family, so they moved.

When she was in Moab, her husband died. Her two sons had disobeyed God by marrying Moabite women, and then they died too. Naomi was out of God's will. She had blown it. She got out of God's territory and lost all that she had. Was there hope for her?

Have you ever wondered, "Is there hope for me?" Yes, there was hope for Naomi, and there is hope for you! If you've blown it, repent and get out of the mess! EL SHADDAI can turn it around to your favor.

Naomi was a defeated woman when she left Moab to return to Bethlehem. But then one of her daughters-in-law ran to meet her. The girl, whose name was Ruth, said, "Your God will be my God! Your land will be my land! I won't leave you, Naomi. I'll live where you live!"

What a comfort! Together, the two women returned to Bethlehem; and when someone saw Naomi, they said, "Wow! Is that Naomi? She looks terrible—She's so aged looking!"

And Naomi's reply was, "Do not call me Naomi. Call me 'Mara,' for the Almighty has dealt bitterly with me."

I used to think "What a murmurer!" But then I realized that she was calling God EL SHADDAI. "Yes," she was saying, "I have been in a bitter, ugly situation. But Almighty God, the One Who is more than enough in a bitter situation, can turn it around and change it!" Naomi used the name ALMIGHTY several times.

What happened? Naomi, whose own children had died, found

a daughter in Ruth. She advised Ruth, who married a man named Boaz from the household of Naomi's late husband. And those grandchildren took on Naomi's name! It may have seemed impossible for Naomi to have a grandchild, but she got to hold that first baby boy Obed in her arms!

And best of all, Obed—her grandchild in name—had a son named Jesse. Jesse had a son named David. David was in the lineage of Jesus Christ! A woman who had lost it all was wonderfully blessed because she knew EL SHADDAI and spoke of Him with her mouth.

Revelation 16:7 and 14 speak about EL SHADDAI. But when I read those verses, they didn't seem to fit with the others:

> *"And I heard another out of the altar say, 'Even so, Lord God Almighty, true and righteous are thy judgments'"* (Revelation 16:7).

This verse continues about the outpouring of the fourth vial-judgment. The ALMIGHTY, the God Who is more than enough, will pour out more than enough judgment on this world:

> *For they are the spirits of devils, working miracles, which go forth unto the kings of the earth and of the whole world, to gather them to the battle of that great day of God Almighty* (Revelation 16:14).

The ALMIGHTY GOD Who is more than enough will pour out more than enough wrath in the end-time battle:

> *And out of his mouth goeth a sharp sword, that*

*with it he should smite the nations: and he shall
rule them with a rod of iron: and he treadeth the
winepress of the fierceness and wrath of Almighty
God* (Revelation 19:15).

I would rather have the blessing of the Almighty than to have
His wrath! Whatever God does, He does in abundance. You
have to make a choice of which you would rather have—
abundance of blessing or wrath.

You can't stand in the middle and choose neither. It's
blessings and abundances or it's wrath. The day is coming when
God is going to judge the earth. Choose His abundance. Choose
for Him to be all sufficient in every one of your situations. EL
SHADDAI—what a name to camp under! Have you staked your
claim?

EL SHADDAI wants to be more than enough to you. **Speak
of Him. Get to know Him, and trust Him as the ALL-
SUFFICIENT ONE.** Here are some scriptures that portray God
as EL SHADDAI:

*And to know the love of Christ, which passeth
knowledge, that ye might be filled with all the fulness
of God. Now unto him that is able to do exceeding
abundantly above all that we ask or think, according
to the power that worketh in us. Unto him be glory
in the church by Christ Jesus throughout all ages,
world without end. Amen* (Ephesians 3:19-21).

*. . . Behold, I will make thee fruitful, and multiply
thee, and I will make of thee a multitude of people;
and will give this land to thy seed after thee for an
everlasting possession* (Genesis 48:4).

*Every branch in me that beareth not fruit he taketh away: and every branch that beareth fruit, he purgeth it, that it may bring forth more fruit. Ye have not chosen me, but I have chosen you, and ordained you, that ye should go and bring forth fruit, and that your fruit should remain: that whatsoever ye shall ask of the Father in my name, he may give it you* (John 15:2,16).

# Chapter Four

# ADONAI

The names you have studied so far—ELOHIM, JEHOVAH, and EL SHADDAI—have all related to the **person** of God. ELOHIM has expressed the might and power of God; JEHOVAH has expressed the holiness and righteousness of God as our Redeemer; and you have seen Him as a wonderful God of blessings and all sufficiency as EL SHADDAI.

Translated in your King James Bible as "Lord," ADONAI is a somewhat different name for God in that it reflects our responsibility as His servants.

The Lord wants to say something special to you through this name. Knowing Him as ADONAI will help you in making a deeper commitment to Him. I get excited about teaching Who ADONAI is, and you will be excited about putting this truth to use in your life.

ADONAI is used over 300 times in the Old Testament alone; and it literally means "Master, Owner, or Lord." This is a name that signifies **ownership** and our own responsibilities that come from being owned by God.

There is an interesting facet of ADONAI that is found only in another of God's names—ELOHIM. ADONAI can be translated as being both **plural** and **possessive**, so it confirms the fact of a triune Godhead: Father, Son, and Holy Spirit. When used to describe men, the singular word **adon** is used. But when describing God, the word becomes ADONAI. It is so exciting to see God, Jesus, and the Holy Spirit involved in this wonderful name. And their involvement is confirmed in the scriptures:

> *"The LORD said unto my Lord, 'Sit thou at my right hand, until I make thine enemies thy footstool'"* (Psalm 110:1).

Plurality in the name ADONAI is further confirmed in this scripture from the New Testament:

*"Therefore let all the house of Israel know assuredly, that God hath made that same Jesus, whom ye have crucified, both Lord and Christ"* (Acts 2:36).

God, as our ADONAI, is in the position of being the Master, and we are His purchased possession. Exodus 21 offers a picture of this relationship:

*Now these are the judgments which thou shalt set before them. If thou buy an Hebrew servant, six years he shall serve: and in the seventh he shall go out free for nothing. If he came in by himself, he shall go out by himself: if he were married, then his wife shall go out with him. If his master have given him a wife, and she have born him sons or daughters; the wife and her children shall be her master's, and he shall go out by himself.*

*And if the servant shall plainly say, I love my master, my wife, and my children; I will not go out free: Then his master shall bring him unto the judges; he shall also bring him to the door, or unto the door post; and his master shall bore his ear through with an aul; and he shall serve him for ever* (Exodus 21:1-6).

The Israelites allowed slavery on a limited basis. If a man were so poor that he could not support himself financially—and was in danger of poverty and starvation—he could approach another Israelite and say, "Could I be your slave for six years?" As a slave, this man was responsible to obey every order; and his master would provide his food, lodging, direction, and protection for those six years. Slaves were subject to all the master's desires.

However, in the seventh year slaves were allowed to go free. At the time of departure, masters were responsible to supply their former slaves with a certain amount of material wealth. If a man had married before enslavement and brought his wife along, she and any of their children would go free. However, if the master had provided the wife, she and any of her children born into slavery would stay behind. But the man could leave free. Naturally, men who were loving husbands and fathers would certainly not want to leave their wives and children!

Should a slave decide to remain in slavery to his master, they would pierce the servant's ear with an awl and plug the hole with the master's coat of arms or a special color.

What did this symbolize? This was the slave's way of saying, "I am a slave by my own choice. I will never be free, and my master has obtained my total obedience for life. I am a willing slave whose master is totally responsible over me." This person was called a **bondslave.**

ADONAI is the God Who totally owns His people. He protects them, provides for them, and directs them. ADONAI is the Master Whose servants have chosen to serve Him because they love Him. This is a beautiful illustration of the Father-Son relationship that takes place between God and Jesus. Jesus came to earth—by the Father's will—to redeem us. He never sinned, because He was carrying out the responsibility that His Father gave Him.

The Bible says, when Jesus' time of physical death

approached, He entered a garden called Gethsemane to pray. The account is in Luke 22:

> . . . *Father, if thou be willing, remove this cup from me: nevertheless not my will, but thine, be done. And there appeared an angel unto him from heaven, strengthening him. And being in an agony he prayed more earnestly: and his sweat was as it were great drops of blood falling down to the ground* (Luke 22:42-44).

The garden of Gethsemane saw a struggle that day. I believe the Father said, "Son, You don't have to drink of this cup. But it is for Your Bride (Israel) and many children (the Church)."

By saying, "Not My will, but Yours be done," Jesus was saying, "I am more than His servant; I am a **bondslave** to My Father's will. I came here to complete My Father's will, so I am willing to be pierced."

ADONAI—Master, and Lord of lords, displayed through the Father, the Son, and the Holy Spirit. Jesus' hands and feet were nailed onto a cross. His flesh was cruelly beaten, and His side was pierced with a sword. Why? Because He became a bondslave to the Father. Jesus said, "No matter the cost, I will perform **Your** will, not **Mine**."

Jesus gave Himself as a slave:

> *Let this mind be in you, which was also in Christ Jesus: Who, being in the form of God, thought it not robbery to be equal with God: But made himself of no reputation, and took upon him the form of a servant, and was made in the likeness of men* (Philippians 2:5-7).

69

Jesus, the bondslave to His Father, willingly hung upon a cross. He was willingly pierced, because He loves you. Today, He still carries the signs of His bondslavery. The Old Testament slaves may have had plugs in their ears, but Jesus' enslavement has marked Him beyond that: He has a scar on His side and on His hands and feet. There are scars upon His back and head. Those marks say one thing: **bondslave.** Zechariah 12:10 says: " . . . *they shall look upon me whom they have pierced, and they shall mourn for him, as one mourneth for his only son, . . . .*"

Those people who pierced Jesus will look upon Him again on the Day of Judgment.

Like Psalm 110:1 and Acts 2:36, this verse from Zechariah also confirms the plurality within the name ADONAI.

Many people really cringe at the thought of God having complete ownership over them. A lot of people have been conformed to the world's image of thinking; "I have to be my own person," or, "I'm just a free spirit." You are not a free spirit! You have been purchased for the expensive price of the Lord's own blood. But even more than that, I Corinthians 7:22 says, *"For he that is called in the Lord, being a servant, is the Lord's freeman: . . . ."*

The only freeing Spirit is the Holy Spirit, Who is in agreement with the Father and Son. It's in becoming a **bondslave** to ADONAI that you will be free **in** Him!

" . . . *where the Spirit of the Lord is, there is liberty"* (II Corinthians 3:17).

*"And unto man he said, 'Behold, the fear of the Lord, that is wisdom; and to depart from evil is understanding'"* (Job 28:28).

*"The fear of the LORD is the beginning of wisdom: . . . "* (Proverbs 9:10).

Job was saying, "Behold, the fear of ADONAI—**that** is wisdom!" To respect the Lord and give Him total ownership is the wisest thing you will ever do. Fear does not mean, in this context, that you are cowering and afraid. **Fear** means "respect and reverence of Him as your Master"; it denotes willingness to make Him the Owner and Master over your life. He wants to provide for you totally as well as protect and direct you—but you must first use the wisdom that lets Him do that. Make ADONAI your Master!

You can receive Jesus as your Savior and still not make Him the Master of your life. In fact, many people receive Him without ever realizing that He wants to be the Master over their lives. But Jesus doesn't want us calling the shots.

If you are still at the reins in your life, then you are not entering into the Lord's fullness. Revelation knowledge of God's Word and victory can only come to His children one way: when they put ADONAI in the place of **control!**

Genesis 15 tells about some people who decided to make God the Master over their lives:

*"And Abram said, Lord GOD, what wilt thou give me, seeing I go childless, and the steward of my house is this Eliezer of Damascus?"*
(Genesis 15:2).

In this chapter God and Abram made a covenant together. God identified Abraham's seed that would number as the stars of heaven and the dust of the earth. But God did not covenant

71

with Abram until he had said, "Lord God—ADONAI, ELOHIM."

Abram was saying, "Yes, You are the God of power and might. You are also my Master."

Have you ever wondered, "I thought I had a covenant with the Lord—why aren't His promises coming to pass in my life?"

I have a question for you: Have you made Him your Master?

Moses was smart—he made God his Master. It is recorded in Exodus 4:10:

> *And Moses said unto the LORD, O my Lord, I am not eloquent, neither heretofore, nor since thou hast spoken unto thy servant: but I am slow of speech, and of a slow tongue.*

Moses said this when he was trying to get out of leading the children of Israel out of Egypt. But he prefaced it by saying, "You're the Master, and I'll do it because You're my Owner. You're my Protector, and You give me direction for my life."

The book of Judges has some key things for you to read. It explains that God wants to bless His people; He wants to deliver them out of negative situations, but He cannot do it if they won't let Him be the Master. In the book of Judges, the Israelites were in a very blackslidden condition. They had taken the Promised Land—but they left the Word (the Promises) behind! They were involved with idolatry and sin, and then everything fell apart.

A wicked king named Chushanrishathaim came to battle against Israel, and his name really fits. It means "double wickedness." Maybe that's why it's so long.

A man named Othniel was Israel's first judge—in office at the time—and he had a wonderful family tree. His father-in-law was Caleb, who was full of God's Spirit. It was a good thing Caleb was still around when Chushanrishathaim came against Israel—the Israelites could have easily lost the fight. But God gave Caleb a special anointing to fight, and Israel was delivered marvelously.

But what happened as soon as this conflict ended? The Israelites slipped right back into idolatry again. They returned to doing their own thing. And this time they paid the piper. The Midianites were allowed by God to overwhelm them. Fires raged through the crops and destroyed huge plots of land. Men, women, children were killed; and their households were plundered. Terror caused many desperate people to dig holes in the ground where they could hide. Others dwelt in caves. Idolatry had once again cost Israel a dear price.

One day, a man named Gideon was going about his business when an angel of the Lord appeared to him, saying, "Gideon, you mighty man of valor!" Gideon may have looked around to see to whom else the angel was speaking, but Gideon was all alone—the angel was talking to him. Full of anxiety, Gideon said:

> *. . . Oh my Lord* [Master or Owner], *if the LORD be with us, why then is all this befallen us? and where be all his miracles which our fathers told us of, saying, Did not the LORD bring us up from Egypt? but now the LORD hath forsaken us, and delivered us into the hands of the Midianites* (Judges 6:13).

Gideon was saying, "If we have such a great Master and Owner, why isn't He protecting us? Why isn't He providing for us? Why isn't He directing us?" Gideon had said the words that

73

needed to be said: Master, Owner, ADONAI.

Then the angel said to Gideon:

> *... Go in this thy might, and thou shalt save Israel*
> *from the hand of the Midianites: have not I sent thee?*
> *And he said unto him, Oh my Lord, wherewith shall*
> *I save Israel? behold, my family is poor in Manasseh,*
> *and I am the least in my father's house*
> (Judges 6:14-15).

The angel said, "Gideon, you are going to deliver your people."

Gideon may have thought, "I had to complain. See what happens when you open your mouth?" He had some real excuses too: "We're poor! I'm a nobody!"

All of that was really untrue, because Gideon's father was once the leading man in his town. Gideon was their key son who had a real future in Manasseh. But that was before the Midianites had destroyed things. Now Gideon had a poor and fearful self-image.

The angel kept saying, "Gideon, you're a mighty man of valor!" to overcome Gideon's terrible inferiority complex. Perhaps he felt so inferior and cowardly that he actually became that way. But when God is your Master and Owner, He will put you over.

Many people think the word "master" describes someone who will squeeze them under his thumb. That is not true of God! He wants to lift you up and put you over: "Gideon, you mighty man of valor!"

God looks at you in the light of HIS Word—not yours! He sees you in the image of Jesus Himself. ADONAI, as Master, wants you to be very, very victorious; so He speaks positive words: His Word! ADONAI wants to protect you and care for you, but if you won't let Him, then He can't. Gideon did the right thing when he said, "Master." Then the words of deliverance came.

Finally, Gideon said, *". . . If now I have found grace in thy sight, then shew me a sign that thou talkest with me''* (Judges 6:17).

The angel was willing. Gideon prepared a sacrifice and presented it as the angel directed:

> *And the angel of God said unto him, Take the flesh and the unleavened cakes, and lay them upon this rock, and pour out the broth. And he did so. Then the angel of the LORD put forth the end of the staff that was in his hand, and touched the flesh and the unleavened cakes; and there rose up fire out of the rock, and consumed the flesh and the unleavened cakes. . . . And when Gideon perceived that he was an angel of the LORD, Gideon said, Alas, O Lord GOD! for because I have seen an angel of the LORD face to face* (Judges 6:20-22).

The Master-Owner allowed Gideon to see a miracle, so he would confess and agree that he was indeed a mighty man of valor. Instead, Gideon showed the worst self-image ever. He cried out, "Oh! I've seen the Lord, so I'm going to die!"

Obviously he didn't realize that the Word of God is practical— how could Gideon be a deliverer if God were to kill him? If fear overtakes you, be practical with God's Word—and the fear will leave!

> *And the LORD said unto him, Peace be unto thee; fear not: thou shalt not die. Then Gideon built an altar there unto the LORD, and called it Jehovah-shalom:*

*unto this day it is yet in Ophrah of the Abiezrites*
(Judges 6:23-24).

Gideon built an altar because God had given him peace. God was still trying to get Gideon to speak and believe that He was the Master of the situation. After this, Gideon became bolder: he pulled down the altar of Baal and built an altar to the Lord.

The idolatrous people got upset when they discovered that their statue of Baal had been pulled down. Then someone said, "I think Gideon pulled this down! We'll kill him for that!"

Gideon's father stepped out. He told them to wait just a minute; he said, "... *Will ye plead for Baal? ... if he be a god, let him plead for himself, because one hath cast down his altar*'" (Judges 6:31).

The people agreed to this; and they told Gideon, "Baal's going to get you!" Of course, Baal couldn't possibly "get him," so Gideon's life was spared.

When harvest time arrived, the Midianites arrived also. They gathered together, covering the valley of Israel by the thousands and prepared for an attack.

Where was Gideon? Although God had spoken to him, and he had seen a miracle, and although God had given him peace and spared him, Gideon was still hiding and full of fear.

Then something happened:

*"But the Spirit of the LORD came upon Gideon, and he blew a trumpet; and Abiezer was gathered after him"* (Judges 6:34).

The Hebrew wording for **the Spirit of the LORD came upon Gideon** says that he "was clothed in the Spirit from his head to his toes." Why did God clothe Gideon with His Spirit? Because Gideon needed it; he was so full of holes!

Then Gideon gathered men together to fight against the Midianites; and God said, "Whosoever is fearful and afraid, let him return and depart." At this point, Gideon discovered that he wasn't the only one who had experienced an inferiority complex. Of 32,000 men, 22,000 went home.

Why would God allow most of the people to leave? Because He was about to show Himself as the Master Who protects! When God is your Master and Owner, He will put you over.

God then told Gideon, "Tell everyone to take a drink of water from this lake. And send home everyone who puts their face into the water to drink. Keep only the ones who take their water with their hands." Why only the men who took the water from their hands? Because their eyes were up from the water—they were watching for the enemy!

Gideon was left with only 300 men. God would **have** to be the Master over this situation! The 300 men went to battle against the Midianite army, and the Lord gave them an unusual battle plan:

> *And he divided the three hundred men into three companies, and he put a trumpet in every man's hand, with empty pitchers, and lamps within the pitchers. And he said unto them, Look on me, and do likewise: and, behold, when I come to the outside of the camp, it shall be that, as I do, so shall ye do. When I blow with a trumpet, I and all that are with me, then blow ye the trumpets also on every side of all the camp, and say, The sword of the LORD, and of Gideon* (Judges 7:16-18).

77

The Midianites were defeated! How did that all come to pass? It came to pass because of a man who called God ADONAI—Master!

Isaiah, the prophet, was willing to be God's bondslave, and Isaiah wrote all 66 chapters of the book of Isaiah. He ministered to four kings and had the greatest revelation of the Son of God that any prophet received. He saw the redemption of Jesus Christ, and the book that Isaiah authored is called the "gospel of the Old Testament."

Why? Because he made a total commitment that said, "God, You be my Owner. You call the shots."

When Isaiah saw the Lord as Master and Owner, he reacted by saying, "I am a man of unclean lips." When he said that, a seraphim placed a white-hot coal upon his lips, and the Lord began speaking about his responsibility:

> *Then said I, Woe is me! for I am undone; because I am a man of unclean lips, and I dwell in the midst of a people of unclean lips: for mine eyes have seen the King, the LORD of hosts. Then flew one of the seraphims unto me, having a live coal in his hand, which he had taken with the tongs from off the altar:*

> *And he laid it upon my mouth, and said, Lo, this hath touched thy lips; and thine iniquity is taken away, and thy sin purged. Also I heard the voice of the Lord, saying, Whom shall I send, and who will go for us? Then said I, Here am I; send me* (Isaiah 6:5-8).

Acts 9 tells the story of another young man who called God ADONAI. In the beginning of his story, he was on the road for

---

Damascus—on his way to persecute and kill the Christians. While traveling, a brilliant light shone upon him, blinding the man's eyes. A voice spoke, "Saul, Saul, why persecutest thou Me?"

Saul said, "Who are you, LORD?"

Immediately, Saul's heart was softened, and the Lord could deal with him. Why? Because Saul said, "You are my Master."

According to Job 28:28, acknowledging God as your Master brings forth revelation knowledge of God and His Word. By calling Him ADONAI, Paul received a wonderful revelation:

> . . . *And the Lord said, I am Jesus whom thou persecutest: it is hard for thee to kick against the pricks. And he trembling and astonished said, Lord, what wilt thou have me to do? And the Lord said unto him, Arise, and go into the city, and it shall be told thee what thou must do* (Acts 9:5,6).

How that must have encouraged Paul's heart! His Master and Owner stood by him. Paul called on the Lord, because Paul needed the protection that only his Master could give:

> *For he that is called in the Lord* [Master, Owner], *being a servant* [bondslave], *is the Lord's freeman: likewise also he that is called, being free, is Christ's servant* (I Corinthians 7:22).

Commitment is essential in order to have results! If you want to be totally free, be 100 percent committed to the Lord as His bondslave. When you place Him in command and follow His direction, you are free from worry, fear, or anything devilish! You are **free**!

79

Nations and history has been affected by people who have said, ADONAI! MASTER! to the Lord.

You can affect your world by making God your ADONAI! Is He your Savior? Then you must also make Him the Lord over your life! The two go hand in hand.

Now I want you to pray this prayer of commitment aloud to God: "Dear heavenly Father, I come to You in Jesus' Name and call You my **Lord**. I thank You for giving me Jesus as my Savior, but I now choose Him as Lord over my Life! Jesus, You take over and call the shots now! I'm Your bondslave, my Master. Praise the Lord! Amen."

Jesus wants to be much more than Savior to you. He wants to be your ADONAI, Master and Owner. Is He the Master over your life? Are you allowing His tender protection to keep you each day? The scriptures offer a beautiful picture of your relationship with Him: the bondservant and Lord:

> *Behold, as the eyes of servants look unto the hand of their masters, and as the eyes of a maiden unto the hand of her mistress; so our eyes wait upon the LORD our God, until that he have mercy upon us"* (Psalm 123:2).

> *"But do thou for me, O God the Lord, for thy name's sake: because thy mercy is good, deliver thou me"* (Psalm 109:21).

> *"For ye are bought with a price: therefore glorify God in your body, and in your spirit, which are God's"* (I Corinthians 6:20).

> *Art thou called being a servant? care not for it: but*

*if thou mayest be made free, use it rather. For he that is called in the Lord, being a servant, is the Lord's freeman: likewise also he that is called, being free, is Christ's servant. Ye are bought with a price; be not ye the servants of men. Brethren, let every man, wherein he is called, therein abide with God* (I Corinthians 7:21-24).

# Chapter Five

# JEHOVAH JIREH

**B**efore you discover Who JEHOVAH JIREH is to you, review the qualities of JEHOVAH'S personality: He is the revealing One, revealing His ways to you. He is eternal and changeless. He is a God of righteousness and holiness Who judges sin. And He is the God Who is full of mercy—our Redeemer!

JEHOVAH JIREH is the first compound name of JEHOVAH to appear in the Old Testament, and it beautifully expands the meaning of JEHOVAH'S name. Genesis 22 is the first chapter in the Bible where the name JEHOVAH JIREH appears after the Lord showed Himself to Abraham on the basis of meeting his needs.

When you discover how this name applies to you, you will know that JEHOVAH JIREH not only met Abraham's needs, but also desires to meet **your** needs. Remember, JEHOVAH is the eternal changeless One Who reveals His ways to you.

By calling Himself JEHOVAH JIREH, He is saying: "I do not change—My ways do not change; therefore, I desire to meet your needs, just as I met the needs of the children of Israel in their exodus from Egypt."

The purpose of learning God's names is not to give you head knowledge of Who He is. The reason is to increase the closeness of your relationship with Him. You should know Who your God is, because He wants you to know. That is why He revealed Himself through different names.

Store this study inside your spirit and use the information to personalize the scriptures. Say, "That's ADONAI! He's my God and my Father!" Let Him reveal Himself to you in **YOUR** existence and **Your** environment to meet **Your** need.

JEHOVAH JIREH'S name first arose during the life of Abraham, when he faced perhaps the most difficult trial of his faith:

> *And it came to pass after these things, that God did tempt Abraham, and said unto him, Abraham: and he said, Behold, here I am. And he said, Take now thy son, thine only son Isaac, whom thou lovest, and get thee into the land of Moriah; and offer him there for a burnt offering upon one of the mountains which I will tell thee of* (Genesis 22:1-2).

When it says that "God did tempt Abraham," don't get the wrong idea. God was not trying to "see what Abraham was made of"—He already knew. He only wanted Abraham to test and **prove** the Word in his own life.

When this incident occurred, Abraham was at least 120 years old. He had walked with the Lord for almost 50 years. Abraham was a strong man of God's Word, and **he was growing in the knowledge of God.**

Faith is not a static condition—it wasn't that for Abraham, and it should not be that way for you. God causes people to **move** from faith to faith, from glory to glory, and from strength to strength. When God spoke to Abraham, He was giving him an opportunity to **MOVE** in his faith. When you receive answers to prayer and get to see God's Word perform mightily, doesn't that encourage your faith? It does mine. That's God's way of encouraging you to take bigger and bolder steps.

When the Lord asked Abraham to offer Isaac as a sacrifice, He wasn't calling him from out of the blue—they had been walking together for about 50 years. They had a covenant relationship! God said:

> *Take now thy son, thine only son Isaac, whom thou lovest, and get thee into the land of Moriah; and*

*offer him there for a burnt offering upon one of the
mountains which I will tell thee of* (Genesis 22:2).

This was **an offering of consecration!** This was the peak
of Abraham's faith. After all, he had waited for Isaac for 25
years before he received him—and then had received him
through a miracle! How many people do you know who have
had a child when they were 89 or 99 years old? But God had
promised to provide "seed" for Abraham, and He was faithful
Who promised.

Finally Abraham had his son, Isaac; and now, God was asking
Abraham to offer Isaac as a sacrifice. What did Abraham do?
He stood tall and didn't stagger at what God was asking.
Abraham must have thought, "If God can give me a son when
I'm 99 years old, He'll make sure that His promise is kept. I
am going to have seed as the dust of the earth!"

*And Abraham rose up early in the morning, and
saddled his ass, and took two of his young men with
him, and Isaac his son, and clave the wood for the
burnt offering, and rose up, and went unto the place
of which God had told him* (Genesis 22:3).

If I had been Abraham, I probably would have slept in that
morning. But Abraham did not fall apart over what God was
asking. Why? Because he wasn't being led by his senses. He
was being led by his spirit man.

Abraham had the wonderful quality of a man who **considered
God above his circumstances!** He didn't leave out a single
preparation that morning. He saddled his animals and brought
along servants to accompany Isaac and himself. He even

brought wood for the offering. **He obeyed** the Lord's request to the last detail.

The offering that Abraham was about to make was one of **consecration.** The book of Leviticus lists the five different types of offerings: (1) the consecration offering, (2) the meal offering, (3) the peace offering, (4) the trespass offering, and (5) the sin offering. The first three offerings were voluntary and the last two were mandatory.

Abraham was making a burnt **consecration offering,** which involves **consecrating one's life.** There are times that are set aside in our lives, specifically for the purpose of seeking God and consecrating ourselves totally to Him. Perhaps you give Him special time by witnessing door-to-door. You aren't required to do these things. You won't be lost if you don't do them. It is a form of **willing commital.** That's what the offering of Isaac was. Abraham was saying, "God, I consecrate my son to you. I give what I love the most to You."

**The meal offering** is similar to our tithes that we give today. The people would bring flour or bread to offer to the Lord as a part of their substance. It was a way of saying, "God, You are my source of blessing. I consecrate my blessings to You."

**The peace offering** was a voluntary celebration of peace with God. Men often brought family and friends along when they made this offering. Our equivalent today might be our **taking Communion together.**

**The trespass offering** was a mandatory one. It was made when one had trespassed against a person. **Trespasses separate people from God.** Don't allow them to bring separation from Him into your life. Be quick to repent of trespasses against others.

**The sin offering** was also mandatory. It involved an offering that was made when one sinned against God. I believe Jesus' Cross points this out for this reason: we must repent of sin in order to restore our relationships with God and others.

Offerings weren't ordinarily given during Abraham's time. None are recorded until the book of Leviticus, except for this instance. This offering, which God asked Abraham to make, was a "picture" of the burnt offerings that were to be made in the future.

While Abraham was journeying toward Moriah, which is a mountain range, he did something that is very significant of his faith:

*"Then on the third day Abraham lifted up his eyes,
and saw the place afar off"* (Genesis 22:4)

The book of Genesis tells of three separate times when Abraham "lifted up his eyes." Each time, he was doing more that just looking around to see the view. Abraham wasn't looking at what he could see with his natural vision; rather, he was entering a "visionary" faith realm. He was catching a vision of what God wanted him to see.

There are times when God wants us to lift up our eyes and see the spiritual vision of what He is giving us. When God wants to give you something special, you must be very keen spiritually in order to receive it. That is why consecration is so essential—it keeps you sensitive to the things of the Lord. I believe that when Abraham lifted up his eyes, he was looking at the promises of God and **considering his circumstances in light of those promises.**

Scanning the mountain range of Moriah, Abraham pinpointed his vision on the mountain to which he was taking his son Isaac to be sacrificed. By lifting up his eyes, Abraham was taking his vision off the natural. He was looking to where God wanted him to look and focusing on God's Word.

What was Abraham's faith vision? Hebrews 11:17-19 tells you what he saw:

> *By faith Abraham, when he was tried, offered up Isaac: and he that had received the promises offered up his only begotten son, Of whom it was said, That in Isaac shall thy seed be called: Accounting that God was able to raise him up, even from the dead; from whence also he received him in a figure.*

What is a "figure"? It is a **faith vision**. When Abraham lifted his eyes and saw Moriah, he saw himself sacrificing Isaac. In his heart he considered the sacrifice to already be done. And he saw something more than that. Abraham saw the son—for whom he'd waited 25 years—being raised up out of the ashes by God! For that reason, Abraham could be faithful to God during this trial.

A lot of people say, "Well, Abraham saw his son being resurrected. That's nothing new because Jesus was resurrected." Abraham believed in resurrection before anyone else had ever seen or heard of it! No wonder he is called the "father of faith." He did not live according to his senses; he lived directed by the Spirit and in the realm of faith visions. Abraham lived according to Proverbs 4:20-22:

> *My son, attend to my words; incline thine ear unto my sayings. Let them not depart from thine eyes; keep them in the midst of thine heart. For they are*

*life unto those that find them, and health to all
their flesh.*

Abraham did not let the Word depart from before his eyes:

*" . . . I will make thy seed to multiply as the stars
of heaven, . . . "* (Genesis 26:4).

*"And I will make thy seed as the dust of the
earth . . . "* (Genesis 13:16).

*" . . . and make thy seed as the sand of the sea, . . . "*
(Genesis 32:12).

He was saying, "I can't have that if Isaac isn't raised from
the dead, because God called him my promised seed. God won't
neglect His promise—He is faithful Who promised, and I won't
let His Word depart from before my eyes!"

I take God's Word literally, and you should too. Practice what
it says each day. If you have children in rebellion and you're
hearing and seeing bad things, don't focus on them. You cannot
afford to let God's Word depart from before your eyes. **You
must hold fast to His Word—your confidence—in order
to see your reward.**

Your confidence has great recompense of reward! It has your
children. What you are to see is God's Word, saying:

*" . . . the seed of the righteous shall be delivered"*
(Proverbs 11:21).

And you are the righteousness of God in Christ Jesus. Let

the Word of God deliver your children—keep it before you!

> *"And Abraham said unto his young men, 'Abide ye*
> *here with the ass; and I and the lad will go*
> *yonder and worship, and come again to you'"*
> (Genesis 22:5).

If I had to sacrifice my son, I don't think I'd refer to it as **worship**! Was Abraham's offering of Isaac "worship"? Remember, he had a faith vision!

If you have a faith vision, you must have a faith mouth. How can you see and believe one thing by faith, while you're saying something completely different? You can't. If what you say is not in agreement with what God says, then you need to change what you are saying!

Abraham had the right idea. The words he spoke were in exact agreement with his faith vision. Abraham's statement became really bold when he said that he and his son would return again to the servants!

**Hold fast your confession of faith.** If Abraham had griped, "I waited 25 years for Isaac, and now God wants me to kill him," it would have been a "pity party." The only one who will be at your pity party is you! Pity parties don't pay off—only "faith parties" pay off:

> *And Abraham took the wood of the burnt offering,*
> *and laid it upon Isaac his son; and he took the fire*
> *in his hand, and a knife; and they went both of them*
> *together. And Isaac spake unto Abraham his father,*
> *and said, My father: and he said, Here am I, my*
> *son. And he said, Behold the fire and the wood: but*

91

> *where is the lamb for the burnt offering? And Abraham said, My son, God will provide himself a lamb for a burnt offering: so they went both of them together* (Genesis 22:6-8).

I think this would have been the hardest part of all. It would have been easy for Abraham to fall apart! Why didn't he say, "Oh, Isaac, you are the lamb." He didn't say that because he was holding fast to the profession of his faith: **for God is faithful Who promised.** Abraham's words created a miracle and so can your words. Faith, seeing, and speaking go hand-in-hand. When Abraham stuck with God's promise, something wonderful happened:

> *And they came to the place which God had told him of; and Abraham built an altar there, and laid the wood in order, and bound Isaac his son, and laid him on the altar upon the wood. And Abraham stretched forth his hand, and took the knife to slay his son. And the angel of the LORD called unto him out of heaven, and said, Abraham, Abraham: and he said, Here am I. And he said, Lay not thine hand upon the lad, neither do thou any thing unto him: for now I know that thou fearest God, seeing thou has not withheld thy son, thine only son from me. And Abraham lifted up his eyes, and looked, and behold behind him a ram caught in a thicket by his horns: and Abraham went and took the ram, and offered him up for a burnt offering in the stead of his son* (Genesis 22:9-13).

Abraham lifted up his eyes again, and this time God let him see a spiritual provision for the natural realm—that is, a physical thing that was provided through spiritual means.

**When you pray, believe that you will see God's provision.** Let Him direct your eyes to the place in His Word that strengthens your belief in Him. The Lord desires to give you hearing ears and seeing eyes that will see His provision for you.

After the ram had been offered up as a burnt offering of consecration, Abraham looked at the place and gave it a name: JEHOVAH JIREH: "the revealing One Who is more than a Provider." This name is actually taken from the verb **to see** in the Hebrew.

What does that mean? It means God has seen ahead and made a provision to fill your need! There is not one trial nor problem that you may be encountering that God has not already seen and made provision to take care of. Why? Because He is your JEHOVAH JIREH, just as He was Abraham's JEHOVAH JIREH. He knows all things. He already knows what you will encounter in your life, and He has a provision for you to handle it.

If you are in the midst of a trial right now, lift up your eyes! Say, "God, You saw ahead and knew that I would encounter this crisis. Now I need Your provision for it." JEHOVAH JIREH will show you what that provision is, because He has preplanned it. That shouldn't be a surprise to you—especially if you are a parent. You would do the same thing for your own children, and the Lord is a far more loving parent than we could ever be.

Abraham was saying, "God already had that ram prepared for me to sacrifice. I spoke my faith, and there was my provision!"

When you speak your faith, God creates what you are speaking. After the ram was provided, Abraham said something even greater about God's provision:

> " . . . *In the mount of the LORD it shall be seen*" (Genesis 22:14).

Some translations say, "He shall be seen." Still other translations say, "the Provision shall be seen." What was Abraham talking about? He was saying, "On this mountain range of Moriah, the Lord Jesus Christ shall be provided as a sacrifice for the sins of the world!" Abraham saw the Provision that would be made for you and me.

The Bible says that Jesus Christ is the Lamb Who was " . . . *slain from the foundation of the world*" (Revelation 13:8). In God's mind, He had the sacrifice of Jesus Christ already settled. He saw ahead that we would sin and that He would need to provide a Lamb for our redemption. God preplanned Jesus to come to earth and be His perfect sacrificial Lamb.

Abraham looked all the way forward to Jesus' physical life on this earth, and he saw God's Own Son. He saw the Lamb Who would die for the sins of the world—JEHOVAH JIREH'S Provision! Jesus Himself said:

> *"Your father Abraham rejoiced to see my day: and he saw it, and was glad"* (John 8:56).

When John the Baptist saw Jesus, he said, " . . . *'Behold the Lamb of God, which taketh away the sin of the world'*" (John 1:29). He was pointing to the perfect Lamb Who would be sacrificed on Mount Calvary—in the mountain range of Moriah:

*Forasmuch as ye know that ye were not redeemed with corruptible things, as silver and gold, from your vain conversation received by tradition from your fathers; But with the precious blood of Christ, as of a lamb without blemish and without spot: Who verily was foreordained before the foundation of the world, but was manifest in these last times for you* (I Peter 1:18-20).

The burnt sacrifice of consecration began with Abraham, but those lambs could only be a **covering** for sin. They could never take away the sin and the sin nature. Jesus, the Lamb of God, came to die and rise from the dead **to remove our sins**—not just cover them. He gave us brand new natures that do not want to sin. Why did God send Jesus? Because God saw that was what we needed; and He gave us Jesus, His perfect Provision. He's the perfect Lamb.

Before the first Passover God said, " . . . *they shall take to them every man* **a** lamb, . . . " (Exodus 12:3). Then verse four goes on to say, *"And if the household be too little for* **the** *lamb, . . . "* (Exodus 12:4). Then verse five says, *"***Your** *lamb shall be without blemish, . . . "* (Exodus 12:5).

The world may say, "We need a Savior"; and that's a start. The world can say, "Jesus is the Savior"; and that is true—but it's still not enough. Jesus has to be **Your Savior, Lamb, and Provision!**

*And I beheld, and I heard the voice of many angels round about the throne and the beasts and the elders: and the number of them was ten thousand times ten thousand, and thousands of thousands; Saying with a loud voice, Worthy is the Lamb that was slain to receive power, and riches, and wisdom, and strength, and honour, and glory, and blessing* (Revelation 5:11,12).

Jesus is **the** worthy Lamb—but more importantly, he is **your worthy Lamb, and mine.** I once said to Jesus, "You are my Lamb, but the Bible also says that You are my Lion. Those two are opposites."

He told me, "You need both a Lamb and a Lion. As a Lamb, I died to free you from the bondage of sin. As a Lion, all power is given to me that is in heaven and in earth. As King of kings, I'll give you power to walk in this life in the fullness of what the Lamb purchased for you."

Jesus is **your Lamb**, and He is **your Lion**. He is **your perfect Provision** for all you shall ever need. Praise the Lord that JEHOVAH JIREH saw ahead, and made provision: He gave you Himself.

# Chapter Six

# JEHOVAH M'KADDESH

**H**ave you ever had a strong desire to have your personality lined up perfectly with the Lord's personality? Jesus wants you to have a total image of Himself living through you. He gives you that image in the name JEHOVAH M'KADDESH. This name, which is first found in Leviticus 20:7,8, means "Jehovah Who sanctifies." It shows the Lord as One Who desires to set you apart by making your personality one with His:

> *Sanctify yourselves therefore, and be ye holy: for I am the LORD your God. And ye shall keep my statutes, and do them: I am the LORD [JEHOVAH M'KADDESH] which sanctify you* (Leviticus 20:7,8).

Many Christians seem to drift here and wander there—not really knowing God's plan for them. They know about the "possibility" of having a deeper relationship with Him. They know about the baptism of the Holy Spirit, and some even may be baptized in the Holy Spirit, but there seems to be no growth nor a real hunger for growth.

Why does this happen? How can Christians walk aimlessly through life without getting involved in God's Word, witnessing, or becoming active in the Body of Christ? It is because there is something lacking, and the key is in this name JEHOVAH M'KADDESH.

The book of Leviticus tells about the people who have **already** been redeemed. It focuses upon the sanctification that should follow one's redemption. This book sets forth the **way** in which the revealing One would have His people walk:

> *"I therefore, the prisoner of the Lord, beseech you*

*that ye walk worthy of the vocation wherewith ye are called"* (Ephesians 4:1).

The verb **to sanctify** means "to consecrate, to dedicate, or to become holy." Basically, it shows JEHOVAH setting His people apart to walk in holiness, because He is their God. Consequently, the Lord's people were to set themselves apart to walk in total dedication to Him. This is JEHOVAH M'KADDESH: He is the Holy One Who demands holiness from His children.

Consider this. Even today the Jewish people are **set apart**. What first comes to your mind when you think of the Hebrew race? Their God! However, in the days of the Old Covenant, the Hebrews were far more set apart than they are today. Jewish holidays, ceremonies, rites, social and political systems—**everything** related back to their God. They were a people set apart.

There is another interesting point about Leviticus 20:7: the people were to **sanctify themselves.** God did not do all of the sanctifying. Within the personality of JEHOVAH M'KADDESH lies the truth that men must choose holiness.

Although it has been commanded by the Lord that we are to set ourselves apart, He will never force us to do so. One man who put off making that choice was King Nebuchadnezzar of Babylon. Throughout his life, Nebuchadnezzar received many indications from the Lord, Who wanted to be Master of his life—in total control. One of the first indications came when three Hebrew captive children would not consume the food eaten by Nebuchadnezzar's students.

The Hebrew children received permission to eat a diet of **pulse,** which is a vegetable and lentil mixture. The condition upon which they were allowed to eat this food was, "At the end of ten days, if we don't look better and healthier than the other boys after eating this food, we will switch back and eat your food."

The eunuch in charge had agreed; and, at the end of the allotted time period, the boys looked better than anyone else. The eunuch was so impressed with their appearance that he let them continue eating the pulse. At the same time, the consecration that these Hebrew children made had wonderful effects upon their relationship with the Lord. He said, "Because you have been faithful and obedient to Me, I will make you ten times wiser than the other wise men."

This was the first witness of their God's attempts to win over Nebuchadnezzar. When they appeared before him and tested their wisdom against all other wise men, the Hebrew children's wisdom was superior. That was the first sign to Nebuchadnezzar. Directly after the Hebrew children obtained this wisdom, something else happened:

> *And in the second year of the reign of Nebuchadnezzar Nebuchadnezzar dreamed dreams, wherewith his spirit was troubled, and his sleep brake from him. Then the king commanded to call the magicians, and the astrologers, and the sorcerers, and the Chaldeans, for to shew the king his dreams. So they came and stood before the king* (Daniel 2:1-2).

Nebuchadnezzar had dreamed about a very strange image. After he was startled awake from it, he could not remember what the dream was. All he knew was that he must know what it meant. He said, "I must know what I dreamed," and called for all the country's "wise men." The men were not actually wise—they were all involved with the occult. When they went before the king, he commanded them, "Tell me what I have dreamed."

"Impossible!" they said. "It cannot be done!"

Nebuchadnezzar was furious with this display of ignorance in his so-called "wise men." He warned them, "If you do not tell me what I dreamed, I shall have you all killed!"

Daniel soon heard that their lives were on the line, so he prayed to God, "Reveal to us what King Nebuchadnezzar has dreamed and show us the interpretation." God revealed both the dream and its meaning to Daniel. The next morning he went before the king and told him what God had revealed. This was God's second dealing with King Nebuchadnezzar.

Nebuchadnezzar was so turned on to hear the dream and its interpretation that he said:

> " . . . *'Of a truth it is, that your God is a God of gods, and a Lord of kings, and a revealer of secrets, seeing thou couldest reveal this secret'"* (Daniel 2:47).

Upon hearing the Word of God from Daniel, Nebuchadnezzar had a knowledge of the triune Godhead; yet Nebuchadnezzar still was not saved. With a revelation like that, one would think that he would become excited about serving God—but he didn't. Nebuchadnezzar's spirit had not yet awakened to the things of the Lord.

Many times, we may try to bring our intellects and bodies in line with God, while our spirit is not in line. It doesn't work that way! In fact, God works in a very opposite order than our human reasoning. First of all, He wants our spirits to be sanctified or set apart unto Him. Then He wants to renew our intellects and our emotions to His Word. Renewed spirits bring renewed souls, which are full of God's Word. Then God's Word brings faith, and our bodies line up with His Word.

Some people would never dream of smoking, drinking, or committing adultery. They've lined their bodies up with God. But they'll think nothing of fighting with other Christians and harboring an ugly attitude toward their pastor. They are rebellious and have big personality problems for one reason: while their bodies and souls are "lined up," their spirits are not! All three must be sanctified: spirit first, then soul and body.

Nebuchadnezzar needed to have his soul renewed. Although he had said, **"your God"** to Daniel, Nebuchadnezzar hadn't called the Lord **"my God."** Over a period of time, Nebuchadnezzar built a huge stone idol of himself. It was huge—90 feet tall and 9 feet wide. It stood on the plain of Dura, where nothing else could obstruct the view. Then Nebuchadnezzar said:

> . . . *To you it is commanded, O people, nations, and languages, that at what time ye hear the sound of the cornet, flute, harp, sackbut, psaltery, dulcimer, and all kinds of musick, ye fall down and worship the golden image that Nebuchadnezzar the king hath set up: And whoso falleth not down and worshippeth shall the same hour be cast into the midst of a burning fiery furnace* (Daniel 3:4-6).

Meanwhile, because Daniel had accurately interpreted

Nebuchadnezzar's dream, he and the other wise Hebrew children had been placed in positions of leadership. They would soon be required by the king's law to bow to his idol on the plain of Dura, but they could not. They knew that there was only one God, the living God, JEHOVAH, ELOHIM.

They refused to bow, and when Nebuchadnezzar heard this, he was very angry. Here were the leaders setting a terrible example by usurping his orders! God had dealt with Nebuchadnezzar, but he had now forgotten all about that. He was only concerned with punishing the rebels who would not bow to his idol. He was so angry that he made the fire even hotter than the normal temperature. The men who threw them in were consumed by the escaping flames. Before Nebuchadnezzar had thrown them in the fire, the three Hebrews told him, "Our God is able to deliver us; but no matter what, we won't bow to your idol."

Although the three were bound with rope and thrown into this furnace, when Nebuchadnezzar looked in, this is what he saw:

> *". . . 'Lo, I see four men loose, walking in the midst of the fire, and they have no hurt; and the form of the fourth is like the Son of God' "* (Daniel 3:25).

That convinced Nebuchadnezzar that these three Hebrew children knew something he hadn't known. He decreed: "Anyone who says anything against their God will have their house made into a dung hill. He is the only God who can deliver people like this!" But the king was still speaking with his intellect. He would still not be set apart, because he had not allowed God to sanctify his spirit.

103

Then one night, Nebuchadnezzar dreamed another dream, but this time he remembered it. It bothered him just as the previous dream had. He said to Daniel:

> *Thus were the visions of mine head in my bed; I saw, and behold a tree in the midst of the earth, and the height thereof was great. The tree grew, and was strong, and the height thereof reached unto heaven, and the sight thereof to the end of all the earth: The leaves thereof were fair, and the fruit thereof much, and in it was meat for all: the beasts of the field had shadow under it, and the fowls of the heaven dwelt in the boughs thereof, and all flesh was fed of it.*

> *I saw in the visions of my head upon my bed, and, behold, a watcher and an holy one came down from heaven; He cried aloud, and said thus, Hew down the tree, and cut off his branches, shake off his leaves, and scatter his fruit: let the beasts get away from under it, and the fowls from his branches: Nevertheless leave the stump of his roots in the earth, even with a band of iron and brass, in the tender grass of the field; and let it be wet with the dew of heaven, and let his portion be with the beasts in the grass of the earth: Let his heart be changed from man's, and let a beast's heart be given unto him; and let seven times pass over him* (Daniel 4:10-16).

Daniel interpreted Nebuchadnezzar's dream: "This has been established, and it will happen unless you change your ways.

You have lifted yourself up on pride and believed that you are the supreme one, when it is God Who has given this kingdom to you. The tree represents your kingdom, and if you do not repent, it shall be cut down to the stump. Worst of all, if you do not humble yourself, you are going to lose your mind for seven years, and you will think you are an animal and live like one."

But Nebuchadnezzar did not listen to Daniel. In his mind he knew Daniel's God was the true God—but Nebuchadnezzar would not receive it in his spirit. Nebuchadnezzar did not want to set himself apart unto God.

A year later, the king stepped out onto his balcony to survey his vast empire. He said, "Look at this great empire that I have built." And at that moment, King Nebuchadnezzar went stark-raving mad. He was kept in the palace gardens, because he imagined himself to be an animal. Nebuchadnezzar's hair and nails grew long, and he crawled about and barked as if he were an animal. After seven years, however, Nebuchadnezzar's heart became transformed:

> *And at the end of the days I Nebuchadnezzar lifted up mine eyes unto heaven, and mine understanding returned unto me, and I blessed the most High, and I praised and honoured him that liveth for ever, whose dominion is an everlasting dominion, and his kingdom is from generation to generation* (Daniel 4:34).

When the king, who had lived as a beast for seven years, acknowledged that God was the supreme One, his sanity returned. Nebuchadnezzar sanctified himself unto God, and

Nebuchadnezzar's spirit came in line with the Lord. What happened? His mind, intellect, reasoning, and physical body changed from being like an animal's. He became a man of God: *"For this is the will of God, even your sanctification, . . . "* (I Thessalonians 4:3).

This verse talks about keeping your entire spirit, soul, and body blameless unto the second coming of our Lord Jesus Christ. God doesn't want you to have little hidden closets and missed motivations. He wants you to be set apart totally unto Him. This is what JEHOVAH M'KADDESH is all about.

How can you sanctify yourself? **Through relying totally on Him in EVERYTHING!**

The book of Leviticus states that moral and spiritual purity can only be preserved through sanctification—a "setting apart." Why does the name JEHOVAH M'KADDESH appear over 700 times throughout the Bible? Because God wants a people who are set apart unto Him:

> *"And the LORD spake unto Moses, saying, 'Sanctify unto me all the first born, . . . '"* (Exodus 13:1-2).

JEHOVAH had already said, "Israel is My son, even My first-born." He had set apart the children of Israel and made them His own. When redemption from sin came, it **set them apart.**

When Jesus Christ redeemed you from sin and the law of sin and death, what should happen? You should be set apart—sanctified from the rest of creation. Jesus, the firstborn of many brethren, wants you to be set apart, **in Him!**

God also set apart a special day, the Sabbath, in which people were not to work—they were only to honor him. A firstborn, a nation, a Sabbath, were all sanctified unto the Lord. Israel's great feasts and fasts, with all of their spiritual and dispensational significance, were celebrated and set apart for the Lord.

A special year—the year of Jubilee—was ushered in after seven sabbath years and would proclaim redemption and liberty for all. Every seven years an entire **year** was sanctified unto JEHOVAH M'KADDESH!

**When you belong to God, you have been set apart.** But you are not just set apart to serve Him with your flesh. You're not just set apart to serve Him with your mind. That alone won't cut it. You must be set apart to serve Him in spirit and in truth!

God called Jonah to be a prophet, and he did prophesy successfully to a certain king. Then God told Jonah to prophesy to Nineveh and tell them to repent. But Jonah had a problem: mixed motivations! He wanted to obey God's call only when it suited him. Although he loved God with all of his mind, his spirit was not set apart. He did not want to call his nation's enemies to repentance. He wanted God to destroy them, instead.

Rather than going east as the Lord had instructed him, Jonah headed west and was swallowed by a great fish. It wasn't until Jonah had some time to think things over—inside of the fish— that he totally consecrated himself, spirit and all, unto the Lord.

A humbled man, Jonah went to Nineveh and preached one message: "REPENT!" The people of Nineveh said, "We want to repent," and they were spared. But instead of being happy about the people's repentance, Jonah went right back to being the person he was before. He sat under a vine and cried because God didn't destroy the people. Why? Because his spirit had not been **sanctified!** He did not call upon JEHOVAH M'KADDESH, the One Who sanctifies. What is wrong with Christians who aren't totally set apart unto God? They don't know JEHOVAH M'KADDESH.

Some individuals in the Bible were actually set apart from their very birth to belong to the Lord. While in his mother's womb, Jeremiah was sanctified to serve as a prophet of the nations to JEHOVAH. Also, John the Baptist was set apart while he was still in Elizabeth's womb.

Why should Christians be set apart? Because JEHOVAH is set apart! He has said, "There is none other than Me; there is none as holy as JEHOVAH." Because He is set apart, His people must be set apart. If you belong to God, you shouldn't be like everyone else—you should be sanctified, different! The key verse in Leviticus, which teaches you how to approach a holy God and walk in a manner that He approves, says, "... *'for I the LORD your God am holy'*" (Leviticus 19:2).

God's holiness changed Isaiah's life. He saw seraphim surrounding God's throne, saying, "Holy, holy is Jehovah of hosts."

God asked, "Who will go for Us?"

And Isaiah made the decision: "Send me!"

The holiness of God totally awed, inspired, and changed Isaiah. It caused him to set apart his spirit, soul, and body unto the Lord. He wanted his life to be complete and whole before JEHOVAH M'KADDESH.

Even God's Spirit is called the Holy Spirit. David prayed to the Lord in Psalm 51:11, "... *take not thy holy spirit from me.*" God's Spirit is holy. How can you not allow yourself to be set apart, when the Spirit of He Who is set apart lives inside you? The Holy Spirit shouldn't live inside an unholy vessel. God's holiness very clearly contrasts the heathen deities—their impurity and corruption of nature and worship.

Israel was commanded again and again, "You shall have no other gods before Me." Why? Because JEHOVAH is set apart. Those idols were not really gods, and the Bible says that idols are a "thing of naught." How can you line up with nothing?

God's holiness was seen by Moses and the children of Israel at the Red Sea when they sang a song: *"Who is like unto thee, O LORD, . . ."* (Exodus 15:11). The very same song is in Revelation 15:3,4:

> . . . *Great and marvellous are thy works, Lord God Almighty; just and true are thy ways, thou King of saints. Who shall not fear thee, O Lord, and glorify thy name? for thou only art holy: . . .* (Revelation 15:3,4).

Glory dwells within holiness. The cry of the seraphim who veil their eyes in the presence of God's holiness is "Holy, holy, holy, is the Lord of hosts." The word "holiness" confuses many people, but I like to think of it this way: when you set yourself apart unto God, you will be **whole**—you will be holy.

When I was a young girl, I had a cousin who was very beautiful, but her parents dressed her in very dull and plain clothes. They pulled her hair back into a severe style.

I discovered they did that because they wanted her to be holy. To some people, holiness is captured in the outward appearance; but it is much more than that. God calls us to be modest; but He doesn't call us to look funny, strange, or unattractive. He just wants us to be **complete**, starting with our spirits.

When your spirit is in right relationship with God, your soul and body will line up. Really, your soul and body are just things that your spirit **wears.** Holiness, a setting apart, begins with the wholeness of God inside of you. Some people are incomplete because they've never known and received JEHOVAH M'KADDESH, Who is wholeness itself:

> *"For in him dwelleth all the fulness of the godhead bodily. And ye are complete in him, which is the head of all principality and power"* (Colossians 2:9-10).

Since God has given you a free will in your sanctification, He will never force His will upon you. You must be willing for your spirit to line up with His Spirit. Sometimes I find that I am unwilling. You may encounter the same problem. What can be done? I have found that the best way to counter those feelings is to go before Him and **pray** that He will make me willing!

Jesus was holy from His very conception. Mary carried His holy seed within her body before His birth. When Jesus was born, He was clean. His spirit, soul, and body were 100 percent in line with His Father, God. Jesus actually became our sanctification when He offered Himself once and for all. Are you willing to wear His sanctification? It is the very sanctification of JEHOVAH M'KADDESH:

> *"But as he which hath called you is holy, so be ye holy in all manner of conversation; Because it is written, 'Be ye holy; for I am holy'"* (I Peter 1:15-16).

What is holiness? What effect does sanctification have?

*But ye are a chosen generation, a royal priesthood,*

*an holy nation, a peculiar people; that ye should
shew forth the praises of him who hath called you
out of darkness into his marvellous light* (I Peter 2:9).

When you sanctify yourself by walking in Jesus' own sanctification, you will shine brilliantly to the world. You can't help but be a light of the gospel. Showing holiness isn't long dresses, dark stockings, and hair in a knot. Some people who wear long dresses have tongues as sharp as razors; and some have nasty spirits, because they are only separated on the outside, not holy on the inside.

On the inside of your spirit dwells a new man who looks like Jesus. When you let Him take over, He'll line up the rest of you. The Bible says in I Corinthians 6:11:

*"And such were some of you: but ye are washed,
but ye are sanctified, but ye are justified in the name
of the Lord Jesus, and by the Spirit of our God."*

Ephesians 4:24 tells us to *". . . put on the new man, which after God is created in righteousness and true holiness."* Don't try to work up your own holiness—you don't have it! Set yourself apart in the holiness of Jesus. The Bible says that when we see Him, we shall be like Him and that even this very **hope** will purify us.

How can you see the One Who sanctifies? In His Word! Do you want to know God's perfect will for your personality today? He wants it to be sanctified!

God wants you to be **set apart unto Him**, just as He has set you apart. He wants to make you like Himself—spirit, soul, and body—so that you will be blameless upon the coming

111

of our Lord Jesus Christ!

JEHOVAH M'KADDESH desires you to be like Himself—set apart in His Own righteousness and holiness. What more beautiful robes could you wear? The perfect personality is one that is consecrated to being totally like JEHOVAH M'KADDESH—"the One Who sanctifies":

> *Thus saith the LORD the King of Israel, and his redeemer the LORD of hosts; I am the first, and I am the last; and beside me there is no God* (Isaiah 44:6).

> *"There is none holy as the LORD: for there is none beside thee: . . ."* (I Samuel 2:2).

> *One thing have I desire of the LORD, that will I seek after; that I may dwell in the house of the LORD all the days of my life, to behold the beauty of the LORD, and to enquire in his temple* (Psalm 27:4).

> *And let the beauty of the LORD our God be upon us: and establish thou the work of our hands upon us; yea, the work of our hands establish thou it* (Psalm 90:17).

> *Whereby are given unto us exceeding great and precious promises: that by these ye might be partakers of the divine nature, having escaped the corruption that is in the world through lust* (II Peter 1:4).

# Chapter Seven

# JEHOVAH NISSI

When you look at your image in Christ Jesus, you must look only at the image that is victorious! I don't know what your weaknesses are, but I know that Jesus can overcome them to make you a victor and a conqueror. God's Word says that Jesus always causes you to triumph in Him. **You must see yourself as being only IN HIM!** Without Him, you can do nothing; but with Him, all things are possible!

JEHOVAH NISSI actually means "Jehovah, my Banner." You are going to discover just how God revealed Himself this way. This name is found for the first time in Exodus 17:15, during a time when the children of Israel were becoming acquainted with the Lord. He is a mighty God! He had sent the plagues upon Egypt and delivered His people in a miraculous way. They had met JEHOVAH as a victorious One, step by step, in every experience and situation.

Only a few weeks had passed from JEHOVAH'S revealing Himself in a brand new way when the Israelites "forgot" all that He had been to them. They came out of a land called Marah, through a place called Elim, and into a land called "the wilderness of sin." They actually began sinning, too, by murmuring against Moses, because there wasn't any food. Then JEHOVAH appeared in a cloud of glory and fed them with wilderness manna. Manna must have been wonderfully nutritious food, because that is all that God's people ate. It supplied **all** their nutritional needs.

After the Lord gave the Israelites manna, they traveled on to a place called Rephidim (Exodus 17). At Rephidim there was no water at all, and the people thirsted terribly. Hunger may be difficult and discouraging, but thirst brings unbearable suffering and torment. Finally, the desperate people began to threaten Moses and doubt God. The people forgot all of the miraculous provisions that He had given them: the parting of the Red Sea, the drowning of the Pharaoh and his host, the manna, and God's presence through the pillars of cloud and fire. The people said, "Is the Lord among us or not?"

The Lord certainly was among them. He told Moses to strike a rock in the land of Horeb (which means "fresh inspiration"), and it brought forth enough water to quench the multitude's thirst.

The New Testament tells you that a Rock that provided water in the wilderness was Christ—He followed the Israelites throughout their entire journey. Sometimes the children of Israel had to dig for water. Another time they had to sing to the earth where they had dug. But, inevitably, water would come bubbling up from the earth.

Eventually, the Israelites came against a terrible foe named Amalek. The Amalekites were not the sweetest people in the world, although Amalek was Esau's grandson, according to Genesis 36:12. The Amalekites were direct descendants of Isaac, but they became a terrible enemy to Israel—a real thorn in the flesh, who menaced the Israelites' spiritual and national life.

The Amalekites were the first nation to oppose Israel. They were both numerous and powerful. As closely related as they were to the Israelites, I would have thought that they would offer support. Instead, they opposed God's people at every turn in mean and cowardly ways. For instance, the Amalekites would not attack Israel's fighting men—instead, they would wait and attack the weaker ones at the end of the line—the faint, the weary, the elderly. The Amalekites were unscrupulous and vicious; and God's face was against them:

" . . . *thou shalt blot out the remembrance of*

> *Amalek from under heaven; . . . "*
> (Deuteronomy 25:19).

> *And the LORD said unto Moses, Write this for a*
> *memorial in a book, and rehearse it in the ears of*
> *Joshua: for I will utterly put out the remembrance*
> *of Amalek from under heaven. And Moses built an*
> *altar, and called the name of it Jehovah-nissi: For*
> *he said, Because the LORD hath sworn that the*
> *LORD will have war with Amalek from generation*
> *to generation* (Exodus 17:14-16).

JEHOVAH swore that He would war against Amalek from generation to generation. Why? Because JEHOVAH is righteous, and He hated the sin of the Amalekites. He wanted to cut their memory off from the earth.

Generations after this incident at Rephidim, which we will discuss further, King Saul was commissioned to wipe the Amalekites off the face of the earth. But King Saul's greed got the best of him, and he disobeyed God. It is interesting to note that, in the end, an Amalekite killed Saul. Why? Because he spared what he should not have spared. What the devil tries to put in your life must be conquered and destroyed. If you don't kill it, it may return and kill you.

The Amalekites were living near Rephidim, and tending their own flocks and herds. They hated the Israelites in the first place, but they were also very jealous of them, so they decided to fight them. When the Amalekites came against the children of Israel, finally the children of Israel did not fall apart. They were not a well-trained army, as were the Amalekites, but the children of Israel were finally learning to place their trust in the Lord.

A man named **Joshua** was standing nearby, and his name appropriately meant, "JEHOVAH is our help or salvation." Moses called to Joshua saying, "I want you to be in command over the army when the Amalekites come."

God told Moses to stand at the top of a nearby hill with his hands upheld. Moses climbed to the hilltop and held up the rod of God that had wrought many miracles:

*And it came to pass, when Moses held up his hand, that Israel prevailed: and when he let down his hand, Amalek prevailed. But Moses' hands were heavy; and they took a stone, and put it under him, and he sat thereon; and Aaron and Hur stayed up his hands, the one on the one side, and the other on the other side; and his hands were steady until the going down of the sun. And Joshua discomfited Amalek and his people with the edge of the sword* (Exodus 17:11-13).

As long as Moses held his hands up in the air, Israel was conquering. But when his arms grew weary and he lowered them, Amalek would begin to conquer. The fact that Moses' men, Aaron and Hur, brought him support and stayed his hands in the air shows something beautiful: they didn't say, "That Moses! Just when we start winning, he gets tired. Why doesn't he get tough?" No! They **supported** him. When you see brothers and sisters in the Lord growing weary or faint, it's your job to restore them! Be a support to them. If you sow it in someone else's life, you'll reap it in your own.

In Moses' hand was the miracle-working rod of God that had

brought terrible plagues upon the land of Egypt. That same rod had closed the waters behind the Israelites and drowned the pursuing Pharaoh and host. This rod of God was more than a mere rod. It was the rod of God's mighty hand: the rod of ELOHIM!

Moses was holding up **the banner of God that brought them victory!** Moses was carrying **a symbol of God's presence.** As long as God's presence was established as the high standard, the Israelites prevailed in battle.

When you hear the word **banner,** although you probably picture a flag, that is not necessarily what a banner was in Moses' day. It was a bare pole with a bright and shining ornament that would glitter in the sun when held high in the air.

The word for **banner** actually means "to glisten, a pole or ensign, a standard, or a miracle." The banner or "standard" represented God's cause. It was **a symbol of His deliverance and mighty salvation** that caused His people to be victors over their enemies.

When the Israelites used the words "lift up," or "rise up," they were using the literal word "banner." JEHOVAH NISSI is the Lord—Israel's banner and YOUR banner; Israel's victory and YOUR victory! Who is JEHOVAH NISSI? He is the Lord, our Victory!

While Joshua was out fighting to bring forth JEHOVAH'S salvation, the rod of ELOHIM was held aloft in Moses' hand. With the Lord's banner held high, there was victory.

As long as you say, "God is the victorious One in my life," you will be on top of your circumstances. But when you drop your hands and say, "I'm defeated; the devil has me down," you can count on defeat. Focus your eyes on the Lord, JEHOVAH NISSI, and keep your hands up in the air, holding

His victorious standard high!

As long as you say, "God is the victorious One in my life," you will be on top of your circumstances. But when you drop your hands and say, "I'm defeated, the devil has me down," you can count on defeat. Focus your eyes on the Lord, JEHOVAH NISSI, and keep your hands up in the air, holding His victorious standard high!

Israel's war against the Amalekites is an example of our own spiritual warfare. The Bible says we have a battle going on—even against our **own** flesh, not to mention against Satan.

The flesh lusts against the spirit and the spirit against the flesh. Although your members may "war" against each others' desires, and battles are going on, God wants you to be victorious! That's why He gave you His Spirit to live within you. God is not a loser, and you should not be either.

God told Moses to stand on top of the hill when Joshua and the army fought the battle against Amalek. When I read that, it reminded me of Ephesians 6:11-17:

> *Put on the whole armour of God, that ye may be able to stand against the wiles of the devil. For we wrestle not against flesh and blood, but against principalities, against powers, against the rulers of the darkness of this world, against spiritual wickedness in high places. Wherefore take unto you the whole armour of God, that ye may be able to **withstand** in the evil day, and having done all, to **stand.***
>
> ***Stand** therefore, having your loins girt about with truth, and having on the breastplate of*

*righteousness; And your feet shod with the preparation of the gospel of peace; Above all, taking the shield of faith, wherewith ye shall be able to quench all the fiery darts of the wicked. And take the helmet of salvation, and the sword of the Spirit, which is the word of God* (Ephesians 6:11-17).

God did not tell you to fight in your own armor. He gave you His armor. And if you'll wear it and stand in it, He will put you over! He's the Lord, your Banner:

*Lift ye up a banner upon the high mountain, . . . . I have commanded my sanctified ones . . . even them that rejoice in my highness. The noise of a multitude in the mountains, like as of a great people; a tumultuous noise of the kingdoms of nations gathered together: the LORD of hosts mustereth the host of the battle. And I will punish the world for their evil, and the wicked for their iniquity; . . .* (Isaiah 13:2-4,11).

Righteous JEHOVAH hates sin. If you will hold high His standard of victory, sin will not overtake you. Other people may come against you with evil, but you are supposed to conquer with good!

Why? Because you are standing tall in the armor of JEHOVAH NISSI, your Victor and Champion. Jesus did not promise you, "Well, now that I've taken the victory, it's going to be a piece of cake for you." You have to **stand**—but if you will, He did promise that not even the very gates of hell itself could prevail against you! He has made you a victor in Himself.

Ephesians 6 says that we are not supposed to wrestle against flesh and blood. We must always remember that God does not give us His armor to fight against people. If we fight against people, we're going to lose. We wrestle against principalities, powers, rulers of darkness in this world, and spiritual wickedness in high places.

Do you want to be a victor over your enemies? Then stand against them in the armor of JEHOVAH NISSI! To wear His armor, you cannot lean to your own understanding; you have to lean on His Word! There is no question that Christians encounter spiritual battles, but you are not supposed to lie down and say, "All right, you win."

God says, "You're not a loser! I am JEHOVAH NISSI: your Banner, Miracle, and Victory, Who **makes** you a winner." That's why you are fighting a good fight of faith. It's good, because you win in the Lord!

> *"Thou therefore endure hardness, as a good soldier of Jesus Christ"* (II Timothy 2:3).

The verb **to endure** means "to hold onto God's Word," and "to stand fast in faith." Why doesn't Ephesians 6 give you any armor to wear on your back? Because you have JEHOVAH NISSI to go **before** you into the battle! He wants to be your victory!

You are not fighting battles in your own strength; you're in His strength. When you allow that strength, which is in you, to flow by relying on Him as your Banner, then you will overcome.

Joshua and Caleb both discovered God to be their JEHOVAH NISSI. When the Israelites were to take the Promised Land,

Moses sent Joshua and Caleb and ten other men to scout the land. I think Joshua and Caleb were the only two who mattered. When all of the men returned, the report of those two men was wonderful: "We **can** take the Promised Land! **We can do it!**"

But the other ten men said, "There is no way that we'll take the land! There are giants in there, and the walls reach to the sky. Those giants would eat us like meat!"

Why were the ten men so defeated in their attitude? Because **they** were not looking to JEHOVAH NISSI to enter the land before them. They were not considering the fact that God had already promised them that land.

Joshua and Caleb said, "Those giants are like grasshoppers! They are nothing to us!" How could they be so bold? They were both considering the circumstances in light of God's Word. They were on top, looking down. Those other ten spies had the wrong self-image. They saw themselves as defeated ones, not victorious ones. They did not see their miracle-working God or His promises. They could only see giants.

Joshua and Caleb saw their own true images in God. They said, "We are already victorious because of JEHOVAH NISSI, our powerful, Almighty God!"

Which way do you look at it? Do you consider defeat? Or do you look to the victorious One?

After the ten spies gave a negative report, the people began to murmur and complain, "We cannot take the Promised Land. If we try, our little children will die there."

What happened? God refused to let them enter the land, because they were not looking to Him as their JEHOVAH NISSI. All of those people died without entering the land of promise, and their children entered the land after they had all died off. The ten spies had said, "We cannot go in," and they didn't. The people had said, "We can't go in," and they didn't go in either. But Joshua and Caleb had said, "We can go in. We can take the land," and they were the only ones of that generation who did enter! They knew JEHOVAH NISSI, their Banner, their victorious One.

After the people had groaned and moaned, and Moses had reproved them, they said, "We have changed our minds. We'll go in and defeat the giants!"

But Moses said, "It's too late now. Don't go up, because Jehovah is not among you." But the people went into the land anyway. What happened? They were defeated and chased by the Amalekites. You cannot win in your own strength. You can only win in God's strength.

After Moses' death, the Israelites battled inside the Promised Land and victoriously conquered the city of Jericho. But then they went to take a city called Ai, and they lost the battle.

Why did they lose? Because they did not ask God how to take the city. They didn't wait on Him to see His divine military plan. Instead, they raced in and were defeated. When this happened, Joshua fell on his face before God and cried, "Why did we lose?"

God said, "There is sin in the camp. You'd better get rid of it, or I won't go anywhere with you." (That was JEHOVAH, angry with sin.) Joshua got to the root of the problem immediately! He said, "Get right with the Lord!" and he straightened out the situation. Then they went to Ai again, and God made them victorious in battle! God went before them as JEHOVAH NISSI.

You will not win in your own strength. You can only win through God's strength and with His plan. In fact, if you receive

His victory and walk in it, the Bible says that you've **already won** in Him, because Jesus has defeated the enemy!

> *... Hear, O Israel, ye approach this day unto battle against your enemies: let not your hearts faint, fear not, and do not tremble, neither be ye terrified because of them; For the LORD your God is he that goeth with you, to fight for you against your enemies, to save you* (Deuteronomy 20:3-4).

> *"The LORD is on my side; I will not fear: what can man do unto me?"* (Psalm 118:6).

What are these scriptures saying? They are saying, "I've already won, because I have JEHOVAH NISSI on my side! He is my victorious One!" The rod in Moses' hand was much more than a symbol. Moses named one of his altars after the rod. He called it JEHOVAH NISSI. He was saying, "He is my victorious One, my Banner." Generations later, the prophet Isaiah spoke about this rod:

> *And there shall come forth a rod out of the stem of Jesse, and a Branch shall grow out of his roots: And in that day there shall be a root of Jesse, which shall stand for an ensign* [banner] *of the people; ...* (Isaiah 11:1,10).

That Rod, that stem, came from the lineage of King David's father, Jesse. Who is the Rod? He is Jesus Christ, born of the seed of David according to the flesh.

The Lord told Moses to lift up a serpent in the wilderness

after the people had been bitten by poisonous snakes. He told Moses that all the people who would look on the serpent that was being held up would be healed from their affliction.

The word used for **pole**, on which the serpent was lifted up, is **banner.** The Lord Jesus said, " . . . As Moses lifted up the serpent in the wilderness, even so must the Son of man be lifted up'" (John 3:14). Jesus was lifted up on the banner—the Cross. That very Cross is not a sign of defeat—it is a sign of victory! The Cross of Christ is our banner, our strength, which He has already won.

Jesus said, "... *In the world ye shall have tribulation: but be of good cheer; I have overcome the world.'*" And in Hebrews 13:5 He says, "... *I will never leave thee . . . .* '" And "'... *lo, I am with you alway, even unto the end of the world'*" (Matthew 28:20).

When you place your faith in the Rod, you can be assured of victory because I John 5:4 says, *"For whatsoever is born of God overcometh the world: and this is the victory that overcometh the world, even our faith."* Jesus is at the Father's right hand in heavenly places, far above all principality, power, might and dominion, and every name that is named. (See Ephesians 1:20-21.)

> *"And hath raised us up together, and made us sit together in heavenly places in Christ Jesus"* (Ephesians 2:6).

> " . . . *If God be for us, who can be against us?"* (Romans 8:31).

> "... *we are more than conquerors through him that loved us"* (Romans 8:37).

Jesus is your Banner—JEHOVAH, Jesus! You go from strength to strength, from faith to faith, and from glory to glory in Him. First Corinthians 15:57 does not say that you can win only part of the time. It doesn't tell you that you'll only be a part-time conqueror.

Many people plan to fail. When I studied the Parable of the Sower and saw the hundred-fold, sixty-fold, and thirty-fold return, I tried to be sweet and humble. I said, "Oh, Lord, I'd be satisfied with just a thirty-fold return."

He said, "Well then you want seventy-fold failure. Why don't you take one hundred-fold, the whole victory? That's what My Word promises":

> *"But thanks be to God, which giveth us the victory through our Lord Jesus Christ"* (I Corinthians 15:57).

> *"Now thanks be unto God, which always causeth us to triumph in Christ, . . . "* (II Corinthians 2:14).

He did not say that you can triumph only in a few situations. He said that, in Him, you're always a victorious one! You are supposed to conquer because Jesus is a Conqueror! You may think, "I'm not very righteous," or that you aren't the best Christian because you've sinned. But you can repent from sin and stand fully dressed in the beautiful armor of the victorious One!

Jesus took all of your sins upon Himself, and He gave you His righteousness. I like this comparison. When a lamb dies, the shepherd removes the lamb's skin and places it upon an orphan lamb. Then the mother lamb, who has lost her baby, smells her baby's skin on the orphaned lamb. Because of the

126

skin that is draped over him, she'll adopt and raise that baby as her own.

It's the same way with Jesus' righteousness. When He died, He clothed you with a robe of His Own right standing with God Almighty. It's a garment that smells like Jesus! When the Father looks at you, what does He see? He sees you, clothed in Jesus!

You have been given everything you need for victory in Jesus Christ. He is your Banner of victory. You can now rest in His Word and know that JEHOVAH NISSI desires to go before you and make you a winner.

You can be victorious even when you pass through the valley of the shadow of death, because it leads into the presence of the Father! You can sit down at His banqueting table, because every trial you encounter leads to a banquet of triumph. And then, the Father will anoint you with oil—right in the very presence of your enemies.

Your enemies cannot hurt you, because you serve JEHOVAH NISSI! He is your protection. I'm glad that we do not have to suffer defeats. Don't ever see yourself as defeated. See the devil as defeated.

The next time you see your face in the mirror, say, "I'm in Jesus Christ! I'm in JEHOVAH, and He is in me. So, therefore, I'm a victorious one!"

# Chapter Eight

# JEHOVAH ROPHE

It is very important that you see the revelation of JEHOVAH'S names in context. Exodus 15 gives the context of how the name JEHOVAH ROPHE was revealed. When God spoke to Moses, " . . . 'I AM THAT I AM:'"(Exodus 3:14), He was saying, *"Whatever you may need is exactly what I am."* Throughout Moses' life, as God met Moses' needs in various ways, God would add names to His name JEHOVAH. God will give you continuous revelations of Himself throughout your life. None of us have arrived. He is always fresh and new. The more I am in His Word and the more I wait upon Him, the greater I understand Who He is in me, through me, to me, and for me! Don't ever get stale in the Word. Stay with it. Each revelation that you receive will always be more marvelous, more personal, sweeter, and more precious than the last one.

The name JEHOVAH ROPHE actually means "Jehovah heals," and it arises from one of the earliest situations in the wilderness. JEHOVAH ROPHE was another way of God revealing His ways—His ways of healing:

> *So Moses brought Israel from the Red sea, and they*
> *went out into the wilderness of Shur; and they went*
> *three days in the wilderness, and found no water*
> (Exodus 15:22).

At this time of their lives, the Israelites traveled by following a pillar of cloud by day and a pillar of fire by night. The Israelites did not move unless the cloud moved, because the Lord was the director of all their activity, and His presence was in the cloud. When the cloud would begin to lift and move, they would follow it. When the cloud settled down, they would stop and make their resting place. The children of Israel did not wander aimlessly through the wilderness, choosing any direction that they wanted—the Lord led them.

In Exodus 1:22, you see that the cloud had led these people for three days, and during this time, there had been no water to be found. That sounds awful!

When you enter tough circumstances, you may think that you're out of God's will. But you may be totally in His will without realizing it. The devil could be trying to slap you around a little bit to keep you from accomplishing the will of God. If you measure whether you are in God's will by your circumstances, you'll miss it.

In the book of Acts, Paul was in a shipwreck. Was he out of God's will? Certainly not! He was supposed to go to Rome, and the devil was fighting that. Don't let circumstances push you around; instead, you push circumstances around.

The Israelites hadn't traveled for three days on their own, yet the Lord was leading them to places where there was no water available. Why? Because He wanted them to know that He would provide for them in every way. No matter what you are going into, God will provide for you and bring you out smelling like a rose—if you'll let Him.

Did the Israelites know about JEHOVAH JIREH? They must have known Him, because JEHOVAH JIREH had been revealed in Abraham's time. These stories had been repeated again and again to the Israelites. Moses knew JEHOVAH JIREH, but the Israelites panicked because of their sense knowledge. Imagine hearing your children and animals crying for water. Of course, it was a very difficult time.

When the children of Israel arrived at MARAH, which means "bitter," they found a huge pool of water; but it tasted terribly bitter. Then the people began murmuring against Moses

131

because they could not drink the water. It certainly wasn't his fault! Moses could have said, "Shut up!" and told the Lord, "I'm tired of this crowd of murmurers!" But he didn't:

> *. . . He cried unto the LORD; and the LORD shewed him a tree, which when he had cast into the waters, the waters were made sweet: there he made for them a statute and an ordinance, and there he proved them, And said, If thou wilt diligently harken to the voice of the LORD thy God, and wilt do that which is right in his sight, and wilt give ear to his commandments, and keep all his statutes, I will put none of these diseases upon thee, which I have brought upon the Egyptians: for I am the LORD that healeth thee* (Exodus 15:25,26).

Moses threw a tree into the water. This is significant. Action must accompany faith. You can talk faith, but you must **walk** it also. When Moses threw the tree in, the water was sweetened, and Jehovah revealed Himself to His people in a new way. He said, "I am **JEHOVAH ROPHE**," which means, "the Lord, your health."

Actually, it is better to have health than healing. It is better to not get sick at all, isn't it? God wants His people to walk in divine health.

Some years ago, the Lord dealt with me about memorizing His Word, so I memorized the book of Proverbs. Through that memorization, I learned a principle about the **life** in God's Word. I was in my early forties when I first began to memorize, and people tried to tell me that my memory was going to fail. They said, "After reaching the age of forty, your memory goes downhill all the way!"

Don't accept that idea! You have the mind of Christ, and His mind does not go downhill after age forty. When I started memorizing, I could learn about one verse each day. As I stayed with it, I eventually progressed to learning 2 or 3 verses a day. And, as time passed, I got to where I could memorize 15 verses a day. **The life of God's Word** was entering my body and **quickening** my brain cells.

God's Word is like medicine. When you take His Word, you are taking in health. That is why God told His people to harken to His Word. God wants His people to be full of His own life. You may believe in healing, and that's great, but there is more to it. You must **receive** healing. And you will receive it only by reading and meditating on God's Word. You must continuously feed upon His Words of life, health, and healing.

Exodus 15 says that you will not have the diseases of the world if you will read and meditate upon His Word. He was saying, "Egypt is full of disease because they are full of idolatry. But you won't have their diseases if you will harken to My Words, because **I am the Lord your health! I am your JEHOVAH ROPHE.**"

Before this time, there were other healings. Once Abraham lied to a king about his wife: "She's my sister." Abraham was afraid the king of Egypt would kill him and keep Sarah for himself. When the king heard that Sarah was Abraham's sister, naturally he thought nothing of making her part of his harem.

What happened? The wombs of all the women in his harem were made fruitless; none of them could have children. The Lord waited until the Egyptian king returned Sarah to Abraham before He would heal those women.

Then, as JEHOVAH ROPHE, God entered into a covenant

133

name with Moses. Moses lived on God's Word, and he believed this statute:

> *"And Moses was an hundred and twenty years old when he died: his eye was not dim, nor his natural force abated"* (Deuteronomy 34:7).

Why? Moses fed on God's Word! It was Spirit and life to him because he believed it and acted on it. Moses trusted in JEHOVAH ROPHE. God's life and health was a personal revelation to him, and he received it for himself.

JEHOVAH ROPHE wants to be personal to you too. He wants to heal you and make you whole! People have said to me, "The God of the Old Testament is so harsh! He's a God of judgment. The God of the New Testament is a God of mercy." That is not true—He's the same God:

> *"Jesus Christ the same yesterday, and to day, and for ever"* (Hebrews 13:8).

> *Every good gift and every perfect gift is from above, and cometh down from the Father of lights, with whom is no variableness, neither shadow of turning* (James 1:17).

God didn't switch personalities between Old and New Testament times. He gave us a better covenant; but He is the same! There is **much** scripture about healing in the Old Testament. King David saw God as JEHOVAH ROPHE:

> *Bless the LORD, O my soul: and all that is within*

*me, bless his holy name. Bless the LORD, O my soul,*
*and forget not all his benefits: Who forgiveth all*
*thine iniquities; who healeth all thy diseases*
*(Psalm 103:1-3).*

Many men in the Old Testament experienced God's healing
power. When Hezekiah thought that he was about to die, God
performed a miracle. The prophet Isaiah had told Hezekiah,
"Set your household in order; you're going to die."

Then Hezekiah turned his face and cried out, "Oh God, I
don't want to die! I don't have any children, and there's no
one who will take my place." After Hezekiah prayed, Isaiah came
back and said, "God is going to add 15 years to your life."
Hezekiah lived and had a son whose name was Manasseh. God
is a merciful God Who heals His people!

Healing is not just for you. It is for you to bring forth in others!
Jesus said we are to lay our hands upon the sick and they
will recover.

When I first started praying for the sick, the devil said, "If
you lay hands on them, they'll die." One night a Mennonite
woman called and asked for my husband to pray for her
husband who had suffered a heart attack. My husband was not
home, and I was sick with the flu. I'd been claiming healing
for it, but, instead, it got worse.

When the woman asked me to pray, I agreed, although my
head was spinning. On the way to her house I murmured, "I
can't believe for healing for myself, and here You have me pray
for some Mennonite man with a heart attack. He doesn't even
believe in healing. I'm supposed to go pray a great prayer of
faith, and I can't get well myself!" When I finally arrived, I
thought, "If I go in with this attitude and lay hands on that man,

man, he'll die for certain."

I repented of my attitude, and the Lord said sweetly, "Marilyn, you're not going to heal him, I'm going to heal him."

The man was lying on the couch in an unconscious state when I arrived. His wife and I read scriptures and prayed together for him. We went to the kitchen to go over some scriptures. I wanted to encourage her faith. Suddenly he was calling from the living room. We rushed in, and he was sitting up, saying, "The terrible pain is gone! I feel fine!" His wife introduced us, and, eventually, they began attending church. Later, he became a deacon.

Numbers 12 describes how Moses practiced healing. When he married an Ethiopian woman, his sister Miriam became furious. There was heavy criticism. You might say, "He shouldn't have married her." I won't discuss whether he should or should not have married her. When others blow it, we're not to be their judge, are we? God knows much more about His children than we know about them. He doesn't need our help in dealing with them. We're not the parents; rather, we are the brothers and sisters.

Moses received the heaviest accusations from Miriam, but his brother Aaron ended up being involved too. Miriam was the older sister who had sent Moses down the river as a baby, swaddled in a tiny ark. She watched over him in Pharaoh's household and arranged for his mother to be his wet nurse. She saw him grow up. Miriam knew about his flight from Egypt and his return. As his sister, she was probably very proud of him.

When Moses' first wife left him, Miriam probably stepped in and took the "hospitality role" as wife. I think she liked being a "queen bee." However, when Moses married the Ethiopian woman, who would take over the duties that Miriam so loved,

Miriam got angry! When she started murmuring, she got over into the devil's territory:

> *And the anger of the LORD was kindled against them; and he departed. And the cloud departed from off the tabernacle; and, behold, Miriam became leprous, white as snow: and Aaron looked upon Miriam, and, behold, she was leprous. And Aaron said unto Moses, Alas, my lord, I beseech thee, lay not the sin upon us, wherein we have done foolishly, and wherein we have sinned. Let her not be as one dead, of whom the flesh is half consumed when he cometh out of his mother's womb. And Moses cried unto the LORD, saying, Heal her now, O God, I beseech thee* (Numbers 12:9-13).

How did Moses know that he could pray for her healing? He had met JEHOVAH ROPHE! Notice who prayed for Miriam. It was the one against whom she had murmured. When people speak against you, pray for them and bless them.

That had to be embarrassing for Miriam. She had been the queen bee. She led the women in a dance unto the Lord after crossing the Red Sea. Then she murmured and got leprosy—and everyone knew why. Here is how the Lord answered Moses' prayer:

> *And the LORD said unto Moses, If her father had but spit in her face, should she not be ashamed seven days? let her be shut out from the camp seven days, and after that let her be received in again. And Miriam was shut out from the camp seven days: and*

> *the people journeyed not till Miriam was brought in again* (Numbers 12:14-15).

The attitude of Jesus Christ says, "I don't care whether you murmured; I am not moved by circumstances; I am moved by love. I love you, and I forgive you." That was the attitude that Moses had for Miriam, and she had to go to him for forgiveness. I'm sure, after spending seven days out of the camp, with leprosy, she never murmured again! But she was healed. Faith works by love. Moses' faith to ask for healing was motivated by love.

God wants to heal all conditions—physical, spiritual, mental, and emotional:

> *"Return, ye backsliding children, and I will heal your backslidings . . . "* (Jeremiah 3:22).

Jesus came to heal those with emotional wounds—the brokenhearted and the bruised. He came to heal people from backsliding and sin. He came to heal them from physical afflictions. JEHOVAH ROPHE is health in every area of life! Jesus quoted Isaiah 61:1-2 in Luke 4:18-19:

> *The Spirit of the Lord is upon me, because he hath anointed me to preach the gospel to the poor; he hath sent me to heal the broken-hearted, to preach deliverance to the captives, and recovering of sight to the blind, to set at liberty them that are bruised, To preach the acceptable year of the Lord.*

In Isaiah 53, the prophet said that Jesus . . .

> " . . . *is despised and rejected of men; a man of*
> *sorrows, and acquainted with grief: . . . . Surely he*
> *hath borne our griefs, and carried our sorrows: . . . .*"

We not only need to be healed of physical affliction, but grief and sorrow are needs that also must be healed. Don't carry grief. Jesus wants you to cast cares upon Him. JEHOVAH ROPHE wants His people to be free of every affliction.

When my father died, my mother had a very dificult time. She grieved for a long time, feeling that there was no point in continuing with life. She felt that she was no longer needed. We children tried to comfort her, but nothing seemed to help.

Finally, one day, the Lord showed me something that could help. He said, "She is carrying that grief by herself. Those emotional wounds will cause people to crack under the pressure."

So I called her up and asked her, "Mother, did Jesus take your sins?"

"You know that He did," she answered.

I asked, "He really carried your sins? You let Him carry them?"

"Yes!" she said.

"Did Jesus come to heal you? Did He take your sickness?"

"You know that He did," she responded.

"Mother," I asked, "did Jesus carry your griefs and sorrows?" She didn't answer, so I continued, "If He carried them, why are you carrying them? If you do not cast that sorrow upon Him, you will die prematurely. I need you. Wally and the people at Happy Church need you. The ministry needs you. Cast the grief and sorrow of father's death upon Jesus and let Him carry it." And from that day on, she no longer tried to carry her sorrows by herself. She gave them over to Jesus.

God has a special medicine cabinet for all kinds of sicknesses.

He went to great lengths to provide ways for your healing. He uses prayer cloths, laying on of hands, anointing with oil, and the prayer of faith. Provision for healing takes many different directions!

If you are hurting in the soul area (mind and emotions), JEHOVAH ROPHE has given you a provision. I am reminded of Jeremiah, who asked:

> "*Is there no balm in Gilead; is there no physician there? why then is not the health of the daughter of my people recovered?*" (Jeremiah 8:22).

There is a song that says, "There is a balm in Gilead that heals the sin-sick soul; there is a balm in Gilead that makes the wounded whole." Jeremiah was asking, "Isn't there a balm to heal the soul-sick people?"

I asked the Lord, "What is the balm that heals sickness of the soul?"

"Look up the word 'Gilead,'" He spoke within my spirit. GILEAD means "praise." What happens when you praise the Lord? You bring JEHOVAH ROPHE on the scene. You bring in healing!

Have you ever gone into a service feeling down? Soon you began worshiping and praising the Lord and clapping your hands and singing. What happened? You received **healing!**

People who abide in praise, abide in the Lord! They live in health. Don't get involved in self-pity and all the other garbage of the world. You don't have to take the "diseases of the Egyptians." You only need to receive the health of JEHOVAH ROPHE.

Jesus was bruised in your place. He came to give you liberty.

When He was hanging upon the cross, soldiers tried to give Him a sponge soaked in myrrh, but Jesus refused to drink it. Why? Because myrrh works as an anesthetic and would have deadened His pain. Jesus carried all of your anxieties, fears, and rejections. He carried all your physical afflictions. They're **not yours** anymore, so why are you carrying them? Why would you carry something when Jesus took it to the utmost for you? He refused the myrrh. Song of Solomon 1:13 says,

> *"A bundle of myrrh is my wellbeloved unto me; he shall lie all night betwixt my breasts."*

Myrrh smells good, and people in Old Testament times used it in many ways: they put it in their clothes, in sacrifices, in incense, and in oil. It could also be crushed into powder or remain in twigs. This scripture is about Jesus—He is not just a pinch of dried myrrh, or a little drop of oil; He is a whole bundle of myrrh. He has a stick of myrrh for every heartache and heartbreak that you will ever encounter. When you allow Jesus to heal wounds in your soul—not just the physical area— you will really begin to smell victorious! You'll start smelling sweet, like Him.

When the Israelites left Egypt, they ate lamb with bitter herbs. We'll encounter bitter circumstances at times, but if we'll mix them with the Lamb of God, He will bring healing.

The three Hebrew children were thrown into Nebuchadnezzar's furnace for not bowing to his idol; but when they came out, they didn't even **smell** like smoke! Why? They were in the fire with Jesus. They did not want to come out, away from Him; and I don't blame them!

Perhaps you have come out of some negative experiences

141

that have wounded you, and you smell like smoke. You still talk and complain about them, and they still show. Come to Jesus, and cast that wound and hurt upon Him. Let Him remove that smoky smell and make you smell like myrrh—like Himself, JEHOVAH ROPHE!

Jesus is your JEHOVAH ROPHE. He has healing for you. He has healing from sin, backsliding, physical ailments, heart wounds, rejection—everything.

No matter what sort of affliction may try to attach to you, you can bring forth the healing of JEHOVAH ROPHE! He never changes. He is the same today as He was when the children of Israel knew Him as **the Lord, our health**. He has wonderful healing for you too. Have you received Him as **the Lord, your health?**

> *"For I will restore health unto thee, and I will heal thee of thy wounds, saith the LORD; . . . "* (Jeremiah 30:17).

> *Moreover the light of the moon shall be as the light of the sun, and the light of the sun shall be sevenfold, as the light of seven days, in the day that the LORD bindeth up the breach of his people, and healeth the stroke of their wound* (Isaiah 30:26).

> *And Jesus went about all Galilee, teaching in their synagogues, and preaching the gospel of the kingdom, and healing all manner of sickness and all manner of disease among the people* (Matthew 4:23)

*. . . Whosoever drinketh of this water shall thirst again: But whosoever drinketh of the water that I shall give him shall never thirst; but the water that I shall give him shall be in him a well of water springing up into everlasting life* (John 4:13,14).

*And the Spirit and the bride say, Come. And let him that heareth say, Come. And let him that is athirst come. And whosoever will, let him take the water of life freely* (Revelation 22:17).

# Chapter Nine

# JEHOVAH SHALOM

T he image of God's peace is one of the most beautiful that God has put within us. In this busy world peace may seem hard to attain; however, it doesn't have to be when you know JEHOVAH SHALOM. At times, the word **peace** is translated as "whole" or "well," and that should be no surprise. Peace is the one quality that all the money in the world can't buy.

There is a saying, "No God, no peace—know God, know peace," and that is true. Ever eluding the world in all of its activity, how wonderful it is that we, the children of JEHOVAH SHALOM, have exactly what the world is looking for—perfect peace!

The Word of God says the Lord gives us an abundance of peace. In this study of JEHOVAH SHALOM, I think you will see a whole new concept of Who Jesus is in your life and heart.

The first revelation of JEHOVAH SHALOM is found in Judges 6. It is about a young man, Gideon, who seemed to have less peace than anyone. First, look at some of the history. Two hundred years previously, JEHOVAH had revealed Himself as the One Who sanctified His people. Since that time, Joshua had passed away, and no central government existed between the tribes, which were scattered about the land. Israel had forgotten about JEHOVAH, their God.

Instead the Israelites turned to the gods of the idolatrous people within the land. The Bible says that every man was only doing what seemed right in his own eyes. As a result of their sinfulness, the Israelites were in the place of great defeat.

The "numberless" troops of Midianites had overcome Israel by using their secret weapon—the camel. The Israelites had never seen men on camels, attacking with swords. They took over the land and burned the Israelites' crops. Why did this happen? Because the Israelites were backslidden from God.

They had forgotten the peace that was to accompany their heritage as a chosen nation.

You remember that Gideon was a man with a tremendous inferiority complex—without much going for himself at the time. The Lord wanted Gideon to fight the Midianites. But, of course, he thought that couldn't possibly succeed—although the Lord told him, "Surely I will be with you, and you shall smite the Midianites as one man."

Jesus inside of you is what gives you strength! Often it's easy to get uptight about the way things look. When David fought Goliath, he was brave and bold, although Goliath was probably towering eight feet over David's head. David could have peace because he ignored his own small stature and, instead, considered God's enormous stature.

When Gideon got upset about the sacrifice being burned up (Judges 6:21-22), saying that he had seen God and was going to die, the Lord spoke beautifully to him:

> *And the LORD said unto him, Peace be unto thee; fear not: thou shalt not die. Then Gideon built an altar there unto the LORD, and called it Jehovah-shalom: unto this day it is yet in Ophrah of the Abiezrites* (Judges 6:23-24).

God gave Gideon peace within his spirit before he ever won the battle. What God does! Peace does not come because of outward situations. Peace comes because of He Who is inside you. God is greater than anything you may encounter in this world. God wants you to make **Him** your peace—not the circumstances. Philippians 4:6-7 tells you how peace works:

*Be careful for nothing; but in every thing by prayer
and supplication with thanksgiving let your requests
be made known unto God. And the peace of God
which passeth all understanding, shall keep your
hearts and minds through Christ Jesus.*

God is saying, "Don't get all uptight about anything. If you
need something, pray, ask for it, and thank Me for it." It is
important to thank God after He answers your prayer! When
you pray and thank Him that His provision has been made,
let His peace **keep** you.

Consider the word **shalom.** People in Israel say, "Shalom,
shalom!" I once asked someone why they say it twice. It is
because they want you to have peace in the inner man and
peace in the outer man. **Shalom,** meaning "whole," shows you
that, when God's peace reigns in your heart, you are whole!

The word **shalom** can also mean "full." You are **full,** lacking
nothing in Christ Jesus!

Another interesting definition for the word **shalom** is "to
pay or render." Peace is God's **payment** that says, "I don't have
to worry about the future, because I know that His Word has
paid for my provision."

A final meaning for **shalom** is so beautiful that I won't expand
upon it. This word says "peace," better than any—"perfect."

The word **shalom** is very important. It is used 170 times
throughout the Bible, and when translated, it simply means
"peace." The prophet Isaiah announced that Jesus would come
as the "Prince of Peace" (Isaiah 9:6). **Jerusalem,** Jesus' city,
means "the city of peace," or "the possession of peace."

You can recall the five different offerings, one of which is
a "peace offering." It was not an offering that would cause them

to **obtain** peace. It was a celebration of already having it. JEHOVAH SHALOM came to bring peace to His people:

> *"For I know the thoughts that I think toward you,' saith the LORD, "thoughts of peace, and not evil, . . . '"* (Jeremiah 29:11).

God said, "I have peace for you!" God does not want you to be confused and torn up. He wants you to be single-minded and full of His peace.

Some have thought, "God gives me many bad things so that I'll mature and be purified." That is **not** what God's Word says! The Bible says clearly in James 1:17 that every **good** thing comes from God!

> *"O that thou hadst harkened to my commandments! then had thy peace been as a river, and thy righteousness as the waves of the sea"* (Isaiah 48:18).

When you obey the Word of God, you will have peace that flows from you like a river, touching other people. Although you may not see victory or feel that a victory is near, you have to let God's peace keep you!

David said in Psalm 19:11 that it is your heritage to have peace. The Lord will bless His people with peace. Peace is your blessing, and it is for every possible situation. How do I know that? The word "blessing" is always used in the plural form. God cannot give you a singular blessing. He is a God of many blessings—EL SHADDAI!

He wants you to have peace that is so abundant that it resembles a great flowing river!

*"For thus saith the LORD, 'Behold, I will extend peace to her like a river, . . . '"* (Isaiah 66:12).

Recall that Gideon had only 300 men to fight the enormous Midianite army. But even **they** were speaking victory! One night, God told Gideon, "If you're **still** afraid, and you're not full of My peace, go and listen inside the enemy camp." He wasn't feeling very peaceful, so he slipped in and listened outside one of the Midianite tents:

> *And when Gideon was come, behold, there was a man that told a dream unto his fellow, and said, Behold, I dreamed a dream, and, lo, a cake of barley bread tumbled into the host of Midian, and came unto a tent, and smote it that it fell, and overturned it, that the tent lay along. And his fellow answered and said, This is nothing else save the sword of Gideon the son of Joash, a man of Israel: for into his hand hath God delivered Midian, and all the host* (Judges 7:13-14).

Gideon heard a man say, "I dreamed that a huge barley loaf rolled down the mountain and knocked down the tent."

The other was heard to say, "Gideon will slay us and win."

Gideon heard the **enemy** say that! Although there were only 300 men to fight, naturally, they did win the battle. God had said that they would, and His Word is never void of the promised results. It always works—that should give you peace.

After the battle, Gideon's relatives asked him, "Why didn't you call us earlier so that we could have been in the battle too? You just wanted to be a big cheese!" But Gideon kept peace with his relatives—even through all of that. He had a revelation of JEHOVAH SHALOM. When you can keep peace with your unsaved relatives, that is really something. It's a witness to them and a way to let Jesus' light shine out. Why? You have peace, and that is something that they want!

When Gideon's relatives griped at him, he could have said, "If you're so smart, why didn't you come out and fight with us? I just did what God led me to do. Are you arguing with His leading in my life? We won—isn't that what counts?" But, instead, Gideon said, "What would we have done without you? You're part of this. After all, you came and cleaned up the whole Midianite army. God led you here, so who are we in comparison to you?"

Gideon's relatives shut up, and everything between them was peaceful. When you are full of peace, you'll have peaceful relationships. Contention takes two people; peace takes only one person. When you let Jesus' peace, love, and joy flow out, there can't be any strife.

There is another quality to having peace like a river. The supply never runs out! Jesus was promised to be the Prince of Peace in Isaiah 9:6. Luke 1:78 says, *"Through the tender mercy of our God; whereby the dayspring from on high hath visited us."* And Zechariah prophesied that this dayspring would guide our feet into the way of peace.

What is to be upon our feet? Ephesians 6:15 says that our feet are to be " . . . *shod with the preparation of the gospel of peace."* God's Word made flesh, Jesus, is our JEHOVAH SHALOM. He'll give you wholeness, completeness, and peace.

The Greek word for **PEACE** is **EIRENE**, and it means exactly, "to live life at its best!" It doesn't just mean "not having a fight." What is your life like now? Is it full of JEHOVAH

SHALOM'S peace?

At Jesus' birth, a multitude of heavenly hosts sang:

> *"'Glory to God in the highest, and on earth peace,
> good will toward men'"* (Luke 2:14).

Peace Himself came and dwelt in the body of a man, was crucified, and arose from the dead, so that **you** could have His peace! Jesus told many people whom He healed, "Go in peace." He knew what He was talking about. When Jesus wept over Jerusalem in Luke 19:42, He cried,

> *"' . . . If thou hadst known, even thou, at least
> in this thy day, the things which belong unto thy
> peace! . . . . '"*

The people of God are to have—and leave—a heritage of peace. What were Jesus' words to the disciples after His resurrection? *"Peace be unto you."*

Paul said that Jesus *" . . . came and preached peace to you which were afar off, and to them that were nigh"* (Ephesians 2:17). Jesus has already accomplished peace for you, because He is the Prince of Peace. Jesus gave us peace with God through Himself, because we were reconciled to God through His death. The Bible says Jesus has reconciled all things, both in heaven and in earth, through His blood. His blood cries out, "Peace, peace." Hebrews 12:24 says that Jesus' blood speaks better things than Abel's blood, which cried out to God in the book of Genesis. What does Jesus' blood say? It says, "**Peace.**" Jesus paid a dear and precious price for you to have peace. How dare you not walk, live in, and claim it?

*"And let the peace of God rule in your hearts, . . . "*
(Colossians 3:15).

You have to decide which way you will yield your emotions. Are you yielding them to the peace of God or to worry? Let the peace of God rule and reign. You are not to worry or be anxious, because JEHOVAH SHALOM gave you peace. He wants you to know that He is in control:

*"Thou wilt keep him in perfect peace, whose mind is stayed on thee: because he trusteth in thee"* (Isaiah 26:3).

Romans 8:6 says, " . . . *to be spiritually minded is life and peace."* When you are upset, you aren't being spiritually minded. You don't have your mind stayed (or fastened) where it should be. Fasten your mind upon the Lord!

Don't let your mind get restless and take over. The root word for **wicked** means "restless." Don't live in that heritage of being carnally minded. Take your heritage of peace from JEHOVAH SHALOM.

Isaiah said the work of righteousness is peace (Isaiah 32:17). The effect of righteousness is quietness and assurance forever. That doesn't mean you seldom speak and then only in hushed tones. No, it means you have a **quiet** spirit that dominates your soul with God's peace!

Abraham called Melchisedek the "King of Righteousness" and the "King of Peace." **First**, he was righteousness. When you accepted Jesus as your Lord and Savior, you became the righteousness of God in Him, according to His Word. Jesus is made unto you righteousness. Peace accompanies that. When

Jesus clothed you with His Own right standing with God, He gave you peace with God—something you never had before! And now that you have peace with God, you can have peace in every situation!

It brings glory to God when you walk in peace on this earth. What a reputation it gives Him when you walk in His peace and welfare! Restless, uptight, upset Christians do not bring any glory whatsoever to God. Everywhere in the New Testament, peace is spoken of as an attribute of God the Father and from the Lord Jesus Christ. Don't take it for granted—they didn't.

You really don't have to ask for peace. Jesus already gave it to you, and it is always available for you. But you do need to claim what is yours. It's not a promise, it's a fact! Jesus is inside of you. You took Him as Lord and Savior, so you have His peace. **He is JEHOVAH SHALOM.**

Gideon continued to walk in peace. When the people wanted to make him a judge and ruler over them, he said, "No, I'm not going to rule over you, and neither are my sons. God will rule over you." Gideon had peace in all situations after he met JEHOVAH SHALOM.

The people changed Gideon's name from **Jerubbaal** to **Jerubbesheth,** which means "God hath put to shame." Did you know that God's peace will put every enemy to shame? Nothing can shake you up when you're walking surrounded in His peace!

Peace ruled in Gideon's life, and it can rule in your life too. Are you living life at its best? Do you have peace in all situations? Peace will not leave you. Jesus said that He would **never** leave you nor forsake you. His peace is better than anything that the world could ever offer:

*Peace I leave with you, my peace I give unto you: not as the world giveth, give I unto you. Let not your heart be troubled, neither let it be afraid. Ye have heard how I said unto you, I go away, and come again unto you. If ye loved me, ye would rejoice, . . .* (John 14:27,28).

Jesus is coming back soon! Live in His peace. Let it reign and rule in your life. JEHOVAH SHALOM is something to have peace about.

You can have peace while everyone and everything around you seems to be falling apart. The God of Peace, JEHOVAH SHALOM, is in you specifically for that reason. He shared His peace with you. He gave you peace with Himself. Now share it with someone else:

*If ye walk in my statutes, and keep my commandments, and do them; . . . I will give peace in the land, and ye shall lie down, and none shall make you afraid: and I will rid evil beasts out of the land, neither shall the sword go through your land* (Leviticus 26:3,6).

*The LORD bless thee, and keep thee: The LORD make his face shine upon thee, and be gracious unto thee: The LORD lift up his countenance upon thee, and give thee peace* (Numbers 6:24-26).

*Come unto me, all ye that labor and are heavy laden, and I will give you rest. Take my yoke upon you, and learn of me; for I am meek and lowly in*

155

*heart: and ye shall find rest unto your souls* (Matthew 11:28,29).

*"And the peace of God, which passeth all understanding, shall keep your hearts and minds through Christ Jesus"* (Philippians 4:7).

*"Peace I leave with you, my peace I give unto you: not as the world giveth, give I unto you. Let not your heart be troubled, neither let it be afraid"* (John 14:27).

# Chapter Ten

# JEHOVAH TSIDKENU

JEHOVAH TSIDKENU means "JEHOVAH, our Righteousness"; and this name first appears in a prophecy by Jeremiah:

> *Behold, the days come, saith the LORD, that I will raise unto David a righteous Branch, and a King shall reign and prosper, and shall execute judgment and justice in the earth. In his days Judah shall be saved, and Israel shall dwell safely: and this is his name whereby he shall be called, THE LORD OUR RIGHTEOUSNESS* (Jeremiah 23:5-6).

Although we know Jesus is the righteous Branch and we know we are in His Body, we often see ourselves as still being unrighteous and full of sin. All of us have felt that way; but if you're speaking words like that out of your mouth, then you are defeating yourself, because they are unscriptural words.

I've heard of people who say things like, "Oh no! My righteousness is as filthy rags!" (See Isaiah 64:6.) In your past your righteousness was as filthy rags, and it would never have sufficed to give you a relationship with God. But all that changed when you came to Jesus.

The New Testament says you are the righteousness of God in Christ Jesus. When you begin to see your right standing with God, your entire life will be changed. You'll begin to move into a new area of faith, and your whole life will flow in righteousness as it never has before.

Basically, **righteousness** means "the quality of being right." It shows the picture of a man trusting in God and becoming the righteousness of God. When Jeremiah uttered the prophecy about a righteous Branch, the kingdom of Judah was in a terrible state of sinfulness.

More than 100 years before this period of time, the ten tribes of the kingdom of Israel had been taken into captivity. But Judah, the southern kingdom, hadn't learned anything from this lesson. In fact, Judah became even worse than the northern tribes.

Jeremiah's ministry began during the reign of a very good king named Josiah. Over the years, there had been both good kings and bad kings. Israel had experienced reformation after counterreformation. This shows the nation's instability in every area of life.

Judah had been on a downhill trend. So when Josiah came on the scene, it was exciting to see the wonderful reformations that he made—especially for those people who could compare it to the time when Manasseh ruled. Manasseh had been a vicious, cruel king who reigned for 55 years and caused nothing but trouble and terror. Historians say he was the king who killed the prophet Isaiah by sawing him in half.

Finally, Manasseh repented, but he reigned only two years as a godly man. That isn't long enough to do much for a country. His son Ammon came to the throne and raised up all the idols his father had pulled down. After reigning for only two years, Ammon's own servants murdered him. For the Israelites to get a godly king like Josiah was truly an answer to prayer.

Unfortunately, King Josiah came to an untimely death, and the whole scene began to change again. The land was full of oppression, violence, political intrigue, and unrest. God warned the Israelites and sent messages through the prophets:

" . . . *until the wrath of the LORD arose against his*

*people, till there was no remedy"*
(II Chronicles 36:16).

God was saying, "I've had enough!"

The beautiful prophet, Jeremiah, asked God to give him eyes that would weep for his nation. He wept over the sins of Israel. He wasn't a smart aleck who went around telling them how bad they were. He identified with them in their sin. He was a broken man, wanting to prompt brokenness in the hearts and lives of the people.

In all of this darkness throughout the nation, Jeremiah prophesied God's Word (Jeremiah 23:5-6). When things were at their very darkest, Jeremiah stood up and said, "This king will be righteousness."

Instead of seeking the healing touch of JEHOVAH ROPHE, the Israelites rejected His healing power, which would heal their sins and their bodies. When JEHOVAH NISSI could have gone before them in victory and been their Banner, they did their own thing. They rejected Him. As a result, at every turn, they were defeated. They would not let God be JEHOVAH M'KADDESH, the One Who sanctifies. To set themselves apart was the last thing they had in mind. So how could God become their righteousness? It seemed impossible.

The Hebrew word **tsedek** originally meant "to be stiff or straight." It can also mean "a full weight or measure" toward God in the spiritual sense. One time, God told the people, "When you sacrifice, don't just give Me animals. A true sacrifice is a broken spirit and a contrite heart." (See Psalm 51:16-17.) Job himself said, "How shall a man be righteous with God? These sacrifices are not enough."

Who is righteous? JEHOVAH is perfect righteousness. The

psalmist said there was none to compare to Him.

Psalm 119:142,144 speaks of JEHOVAH TSIDKENU:

> *Thy righteousness is an everlasting righteousness, and thy law is the truth. The righteousness of thy testimonies is everlasting: give me understanding, and I shall live.*

God is saying, "I am righteous, and children are like their parents. If you are going to be My children, you will be righteous also."

The Israelites were so tangled up with their sacrifices and the fact that Abraham was their father, that they never thought about God making them righteous. They thought their actions could be their righteousness.

If you don't smoke, drink, curse, murder, nor commit adultery, does that put you in right standing with God? Isaiah 64:6 says that your own righteousness is disgusting to God. It is like filthy rags.

The apostle Paul had been extremely proud of his merit. He was from the tribe of Benjamin and had studied at the feet of Gamaliel, a doctor of the law. But after his conversion, Paul said that he had been the **worst** of all sinners:

> *"Christ Jesus came into the world to save sinners; of whom I am chief"* (I Timothy 1:15).

> *"The heart is deceitful above all things, and desperately wicked: who can know it?"* (Jeremiah 17:9).

> *"How then can man be justified* (righteous) *with God? or how can he be clean that is born of a woman?"* (Job 25:4).

You may do every imaginable thing correctly, but there is still sin in your spirit, unless you have met JEHOVAH TSIDKENU—the Lord Who will be your righteousness. No other person could ever redeem you:

> *"None of them can by any means redeem his brother, nor give to God a ransom for him"* (Psalm 49:7).

Only the righteous Servant, found in Isaiah 53, could pay for your ransom. He is the holy One of Israel. He is the Branch of David. He is your Righteousness in person.

What does that mean to you? Peter called Jesus the "holy One," and the "righteous One." The psalmist said, "There will be One Who will cover all their sins."

> *I will greatly rejoice in the LORD* [JEHOVAH], *my soul shall be joyful in my God; for he hath clothed me with the garments of salvation, he hath covered me with the robe of righteousness, as a bridegroom decketh himself with ornaments, and as a bride adorneth herself with her jewels* (Isaiah 61:10).

He was saying, "There is a Messiah coming Who will be righteous Himself. He will make me righteous by clothing me in His Own righteousness." **He'll exchange my filthy rags for a beautiful robe of righteousness.**

Are you in Jesus Christ—as a part of His own Body—because

you've confessed Him with your mouth and believed upon Him in your heart?

> *Therefore if any man be in Christ, he is a new creature: old things are passed away; behold, all things are become new. And all things are of God, who hath reconciled us to himself by Jesus Christ, and hath given to us the ministry of reconciliation; .... For he hath made him to be sin for us, who knew no sin; that we might be made the righteousness of God in him* (II Corinthians 5:17,18,21).

You are a new creature in Christ Jesus, and you are made His righteousness. Not only do you have the righteous Branch and JEHOVAH TSIDKENU, but also He made you into **TSIDKENU!** That new creature is not an old mattress that's been renovated; rather, you are a brand new species. You are a creation that has never existed. Jesus remade you into the righteousness of God in Him to fulfill a part that no one else can fulfill.

Sometimes, just saying, "I am the righteousness of God!" makes me feel and act better. When you start saying who you are, you start acting like who you are. Until you realize what Jesus Christ has created you to be, you will be a defeated Christian.

Ephesians 4:24,25 says that you are actively to receive Jesus' righteousness:

> *And that ye put on the new man, which after God is created in righteousness and true holiness. Wherefore putting away lying, speak every man*

*truth with his neighbour; for we are members one of another.*

You must decide to put on the new man who is clothed in Jesus' righteousness. God is not going to force you to act like a new creature. Every day you must say, "I am a new man. I'm a new creation. I'm the righteousness of God in Christ Jesus."

It is really true that our righteousness is as filthy rags as Isaiah said? Our pasts are as filthy rags, but Jesus swapped with us: He took our sins and destroyed the powers of darkness. Then He gave us His righteousness.

No wonder every promise in the Bible is ours! No wonder He saw fit to renew our minds in it! There is no condemnation to those who are in Christ Jesus, because they are clothed in His right standing with God.

Say to yourself, "I am partaking of the Lord's divine nature, which has never sinned. I am partaking of His righteousness." God no longer looks at you through your sins. Now He looks at you through the righteousness of His Son, Jesus Christ:

*Confess your faults one to another, and pray one for another, that ye may be healed. The effectual fervent prayer of a **righteous** man availeth much* (James 5:16).

Who is a righteous man? A righteous man is one who is born again into Jesus' righteousness. **That righteous man's prayers avail much!**

Jesus' righteousness will cause your prayers to avail much. His righteousness covers your spirit, personality, mind, and emotions. You can command your body and soul to shape up and get in line with God's Word. Tell them, "You start acting like your Father, JEHOVAH TSIDKENU!"

You might ask, "What about the sins I committed in the past?" The Bible says your old life is dead. Your past is dead, so leave it alone.

Paul had a bold confession of faith:

> *I am crucified with Christ: nevertheless I live; yet not I, but Christ liveth in me: and the life which I now live in the flesh I live by the faith of the Son of God, who loved me, and gave himself for me* (Galatians 2:20).

Jesus is made unto you wisdom **and** righteousness. A lot of people claim His wisdom, but they don't say anything about His righteousness. You need both:

> *"But he that is joined unto the Lord is one spirit"* (I Corinthians 6:17).

It is a miracle to be able to partake of the very Spirit of Jesus. It is His Spirit, the Holy Spirit, Who causes you to be His righteousness and, therefore, causes you to overcome death and the grave itself!

> *"O death, where is thy sting? O grave, where is thy victory?"* (I Corinthians 15:55).

Sometimes it's easy to get glum. Maybe you have fought with your spouse or screamed at the children. Perhaps something dreadful went wrong at work, or you just had a bad day.

165

During those times, if someone came up and said, "You're the righteousness of God," you would say, "I'm anything but the righteousness of God!"

But when we repent of attitude sins and sins against others, what happens? Does He take us back, and are we still righteous? First John 1:9 says that when we confess our sins, the Lord is faithful and just to forgive us and to **cleanse** us from all unrighteousness! Repentance brings cleansing.

But even better than always repenting and being cleansed is what Paul said in I Corinthians 15:34:

> *"Awake to righteousness, and sin not; for some have not the knowledge of God: I speak this to your shame."*

Awaken to your righteousness! Put on that image, and let it shine out of you and reach others for the kingdom of God. You have been born anew into God's righteousness. When you see yourself as a sinner, you'll keep entering areas of sin. When you see yourself as righteous and complete in Jesus Christ, you'll avoid those areas. You'll resist the enemy's attacks.

Manasseh was one of the worst men in the Bible. He was a real thug! During his 55 year reign over Israel, Manasseh did every evil thing that he could do. He built idols and got Israel involved in Baal worship again. He set up horoscopes and astrology. He made a graven image and put it in the holy of holies where God's presence had been seen.

When people opposed Manasseh, he turned lions against them. When the prophet Isaiah opposed Manasseh, of course, Isaiah was put to death. Manasseh even passed his own children through fire as sacrifices to an idol. What a wicked king!

God dealt with Manasseh in a severe way. God sent the Assyrian army against him. Manasseh was taken captive and put into a Babylonian prison, where he was very mistreated. The Bible says that while Manasseh was in affliction, he prayed and repented before God.

Then God cleansed him of his sins and sent him back to his throne in Jerusalem. The last two years of Manasseh's reign were tremendous. He took down all of the idols, cleaned out the temple, and called the nation to worship JEHOVAH God.

Manasseh was once a very wicked man, but what is he today? He is the righteousness of God in Christ Jesus. I think when he arrived in heaven, the first person he looked up was Isaiah. He probably said, "Hey, Isaiah, I'm the man who cut you in half."

Isaiah probably said, "Don't worry about it, Manasseh. You repented of your sin, and for me, it was just a shortcut to glory."

Have you cut any prophets in half lately? Have you killed any Christians, like the apostle Paul once did? When he repented, Paul became God's righteousness, because God cleansed him.

The Bible says, *"Let this mind be in you, which was also in Christ Jesus"* (Philippians 2:5). What mind is that? It is His righteous mind! You can think and act rightly because of Jesus in you.

The prodigal son spent all that was his. When he returned home, one of the things his father gave him was a robe. His father said, "Give my son the best robe." The best is always the robe that the father wore.

That son, who had been living with pigs and had wasted his father's provision for him, was given the best robe. When you came to Jesus, the Father gave you the best robe, the one that He wears—**righteousness.** God takes prodigals—those who

167

have spent all He has given them and have ripped up their privileges—and He **cleanses them and clothes them in His righteousness.** That's what **you** are clothed in, and it came out of heaven's wardrobe.

You will never buy a more expensive robe than the one that the Lord gave you. It was paid for with Jesus' blood. You will never wear a more beautiful nor original creation. It is the righteousness of the Father and Son Themselves.

Jesus triumphed over Satan in three areas. First, in the wilderness, Jesus overcame him by saying, "It is written." Satan had to obey the Word of God. Next, on the cross, Jesus stripped Satan of his power. Jesus overcame sin and took the keys of hell and death. And, finally, at your new birth, Jesus won again. He defeated Satan by making you and me—and all of mankind—victors over sin and death.

You are victorious over Satan today, because Jesus gave you His own righteousness—if you've received Him. Don't ever say that you are unrighteous. You are not a poor, lost sinner! You were once, but now you are the righteousness of God. **He is JEHOVAH TSIDKENU, the Lord YOUR Righteousness.** Say it! Claim it! A precious price was paid for that robe you are wearing. Don't deny that you are clothed in it.

That righteous robe gives you prayer power. Pray up a storm, because you have a force and strength to bring tremendous results—His righteousness. **Pray in it, walk in it, live in the beautiful robe that was bought for you by JEHOVAH TSIDKENU.**

What a wonderful name—JEHOVAH TSIDKENU! It reveals the fullness of the measure of our acceptance in the presence of God. How wonderful to have been able to put off the filthy rags of the old man! Now we are dressed in Jesus Himself by

His wonderful Spirit—in righteousness! Have you dressed yourself in the free gift of JEHOVAH TSIDKENU—His righteousness?

> *But God be thanked, that ye were the servants of sin, but ye have obeyed from the heart that form of doctrine which was delivered you. Being then made free from sin, ye became the servants of righteousness* (Romans 6:17,18).

> *For they being ignorant of God's righteousness, and going about to establish their own righteousness, have not submitted themselves unto the righteousness of God. For Christ is the end of the law for righteousness to every one that believeth* (Romans 10:3,4).

> *"But of him are ye in Christ Jesus, who of God is made unto us wisdom, and righteousness, and sanctification, and redemption"* (I Corinthians 1:30).

> *He shall see of the travail of his soul, and shall be satisfied: by his knowledge shall my righteous servant justify many; for he shall bear their iniquities* (Isaiah 53:11).

# Chapter Eleven

# JEHOVAH ROHI

The name JEHOVAH ROHI means "JEHOVAH, my Shepherd." The enemy likes to tell Christians that they can neither find nor know God's will. Have you ever felt that way? Have you ever heard anyone say, "If I could ever find the will of God . . . . " Some Christians wander through their spiritual walks, always searching for His will, yet never finding quite what it is. Why? They do not know the Lord as JEHOVAH ROHI: JEHOVAH, their Shepherd.

In Psalm 23 David said, "The LORD is my shepherd," and David proceeded to give a very personal portrayal of JEHOVAH ROHI. When you study this name, don't think of Him as "every Christian's Shepherd." **Instead, think of Him as YOUR Shepherd, Who wants you to know His will.**

Personalize the scriptures in this study and make them your own. Psalm 23 was written by David, the shepherd boy who became Israel's king and a "type" of our Great Shepherd—the Lord Jesus Christ.

The word **shepherd** has a number of meanings, and you are going to see both how they apply to Jesus and how He leads and guides you. So don't walk around saying, "I never know the will of God." You **can** know, because He lives inside of you. He wants you to know what His will is for you.

The primary meaning of the word **rohi** is "to feed." This word was first used when Joseph fed the flock with his brothers in Genesis 37:2. When the Pharaoh learned that Joseph's family was moving to Egypt, Joseph said, " . . . *Thy servants are shepherds, both we, and also our father. . . . servants have no pasture for their flocks . . . * " (Genesis 47:3,4). Joseph and King David were both great leaders of Israel who began as shepherds.

A second meaning of the word **rohi** indicates "the relationship between a prince (leader) and his people." The

172

tribes of Israel said to David:

> ... *thou wast he that leddest out and broughtest in Israel: and the LORD said to thee, Thou shalt feed my people Israel, and thou shalt be a captain over Israel* (II Samuel 5:2).

David was to lead his people; He was their "leader" or "director."

The word **rohi** can also signify "the relationship between a priest or prophet and his people." JEHOVAH God promised the nation of Judah:

> "'... *I will give you pastors according to mine heart, which shall feed you with knowledge and understanding*'" (Jeremiah 3:15).

JEHOVAH God promised to give you pastors who will feed you with knowledge of the Word. They will explain it to you so that you can understand it. After that, you have a responsibility to apply the Word that you have learned to your own life. When you understand what the Word says, then you are to **let it become a practical reality in your everyday life.**

The word **rohi** can be used with regard to folly and judgment. JEHOVAH ROHI wants to lead you away from folly:

> "... *the mouth of fools feedeth on foolishness*" (Proverbs 15:14).

An idolater, in his folly, "... *feedeth on ashes*" (Isaiah 44:20).

Ephraim, full of lies and deceit, *". . . feedeth on wind, . . ."* (Hosea 12:1).

Ezekiel 34:16 says that JEHOVAH will feed false shepherds with judgment. All of these verses relate to the word **rohi** in "feeding."

Throughout this study on the name JEHOVAH ROHI, you will see how the word **rohi** relates to your relationship with the Lord. Many times, it has to do with feeding.

A beautiful translation of **rohi** is "companion" or "friend." This expresses the idea of intimacy and sharing life and food. Jesus is our great Shepherd, and we are very intimate with Him. The Bible says we are joint heirs with Him (Romans 8:17); we are to share in His life and identify completely with Him. Exodus 33:11 spoke of a **rohi** relationship between the Lord and Moses—*"And the LORD spake unto Moses face to face, as a man speaketh unto his friend . . . ."*

God wants to be that intimate in His relationship with you. **Jesus is your friend that sticks closer than a brother—** that is your **rohi** relationship with Him.

When you see the Lord as your Shepherd, remember all that it involves: He will lead you, feed you, bring judgment, and keep you from folly. He is your close and intimate companion and friend.

The highest aspect of your relationship with the Lord is that JEHOVAH—this very close One—has redeemed you. He has led you out of sin, and He desires to continue leading you away from sin.

God said to David, "As your Shepherd, I took you out and chose you, David, to feed Jacob this people and Israel their inheritance." JEHOVAH fed His flock according to the integrity of His heart. God wants to feed you with goodness and lead you away from wild grass or oats that would harm you. He is your Shepherd.

The Lord also shows how **you** are to lead, as you take His hand in yours. He is your perfect example:

> *Behold, the Lord GOD will come with strong hand, and his arm shall rule for him: behold, his reward is with him, and his work before him. He shall feed his flock like a shepherd: he shall gather the lambs with his arm, and carry them in his bosom, and shall gently lead those that are with young* (Isaiah 40:10-11).

That scripture shows God's strength, but it also shows His tenderness—a part of His image in you. When you are leading others, you are to show both of those qualities. You can discern a false shepherd by being aware of the qualities of a true shepherd.

The true shepherd will seek that which is lost. He will bring again that which was driven away and bind up that which was broken. He will strengthen that which was sick. God said that He would search out false shepherds and drive them away.

A person who tries to cause division in a church is not a true shepherd. If a person is not strengthening the sick and unhappy—if he makes them unhappy and wounds them—then he is not a true shepherd.

One time, a man came to my husband and me and said, "I am a watcher of the sheep, and there are some things that I don't like in the church. I am a member, but I'm going to withdraw until they get straightened out." The Bible says that when the wolf comes, the false shepherd runs off!

When there is trouble in a church, the people who run away from it aren't true shepherds. A true shepherd will stay in there and drive the wolves out. The Bible gives you valuable patterns with which to judge yourself. If you will judge yourself accordingly, then you won't have to be judged.

In Genesis 49:24, Jacob called JEHOVAH ROHI, "The mighty God, the Shepherd":

> *But his bow abode in strength, and the arms of his hands were made strong by the hands of the mighty God of Jacob; (from thence is the shepherd, the stone of Israel).*

> *"He shall feed his flock like a shepherd: ... and shall gently lead those that are with young"* (Isaiah 40:11).

These two descriptions are both combinations of the strength and gentleness of the Lord. There are times when your pastor may need to be very strong. There are also times when he will be very gentle. Likewise, there are times when Jesus inside of you will be very strong handed with you. But His strength is always loving! He is a gentle Shepherd, and that is His image in you. Everything that the shepherd is to sheep, JEHOVAH ROHI is toward you:

> *"And I will dwell among the children of Israel, ... "* (Exodus 29:45).

The word **dwell** is the Hebrew word **shakan**, which denotes the glorious presence of God. Jesus in you is greater than he that is in the world, because JEHOVAH, the Shepherd, offers the intimacy of His presence. His presence is glorious!

You have the glory of JEHOVAH living within you. When you look at yourself, see His glory. If you've been seeing defeat, you've been looking at the wrong image. The Lord wants to reveal Himself through you, and He is anything but defeated! JEHOVAH ROHI is your Shepherd. He knows you intimately:

> *"Thou knowest my downsitting and mine uprising, thou understandest my thought afar off"* (Psalm 139:2).

The psalmist was saying, "You know exactly where I am and how to take care of me. You are leading and guiding me."

I found some of the most beautiful examples of the Good Shepherd in John 10:11:

> *"'I am the good shepherd: the good shepherd giveth his life for the sheep.'"*

The word **good** actually means "appealing." Jesus in you is appealing; He is irresistible! **When you let the image of your Good Shepherd shine through, He'll make YOU irresistible!** That is why Jesus said:

> *"'And I, if I be lifted up from the earth, will draw all men unto me'"* (John 12:32).

People cannot resist the appeal of JEHOVAH ROHI. Ezekiel said about Jesus:

> *. . . Behold, I, even I, will both search my sheep,*

177

> *and seek them out . . . . and will deliver them . . . .*
> *I will feed them in a good pasture, . . . I will cause*
> *them to lie down, . . . . I will seek that which*
> *was lost, and bring again that which was driven*
> *away, and will bind up that which was broken,*
> *and will strengthen that which was sick: . . .*
> (Ezekiel 34:11,12,14-16).

That is exactly what Jesus did for mankind. He came to earth and said, "I am the Good Shepherd. My sheep will know Me, because I call them by name. I'll lead them and take care of them. I'll never leave nor forsake them!"

Jesus told Peter. "Feed My lambs, feed My sheep." That was the Good Shepherd speaking to the "under-shepherd." Peter reminds us that we had all gone astray like lost sheep—but we've returned to Him Who is the Shepherd and Bishop of our souls! Sheep can get lost more quickly than any other animal. But when we were astray, Jesus led us back to take care of us.

Jesus is the Shepherd; but first, He had to become the sacrificial Lamb. Sheep that follow the shepherd become well acquainted with him according to how much time they spend together.

Jesus called you by name. You know Him because you recognize His voice. Although a shepherd may not have been a sheep—and not know what they think—it's different with Jesus. He came to earth and lived as a sheep; He became **the sacrificial Lamb;** and therefore, He knows you intimately.

He came down to earth and showed us mercy. The word for **mercy** is **checed** which means "to climb into someone's skin and look out of his eyes, hear out of his ears, and feel what he feels." Jesus walked in the flesh. He was tempted every way you could possibly be tempted, and He suffered in every way you could possibly suffer.

Why? He climbed into your skin so that He could experience exactly what you'll experience. Then He could give you His mercy! Who could be a better Shepherd than One Who has been a sheep? Imagine the rejoicing in John the Baptist's heart when he pointed and said, in effect, "Look! There is the Lamb of God Who will take away the sins of the world!" (See John 1:29.)

A shepherd never becomes separated from his sheep; he protects them from all danger:

> *The thief cometh not, but for to steal, and to kill, and to destroy: I am come that they might have life, and that they might have it more abundantly. I am the good shepherd: the good shepherd giveth his life for the sheep. I am the good shepherd, and know my sheep, and am known of mine* (John 10:10,11,14).

Revelation 7:15-17 talks about the Lamb and the Shepherd combination:

> *Therefore are they before the throne of God, and serve him day and night in his temple: and he that sitteth on the throne shall dwell among them. They shall hunger no more, neither thirst any more; neither shall the sun light on them, nor any heat. For the Lamb which is in the midst of the throne shall feed them, and shall lead them unto living fountains of waters: and God shall wipe away all tears from their eyes.*

Jesus, the Lamb, is your Shepherd! Do you see Who JEHOVAH ROHI is inside you? He knows how you feel, because He walked in the flesh. He has looked out from your eyes, heard from your ears, and felt all that you feel. He knows exactly how to lead you. He is inside of you specifically to feed, lead, and keep you from trouble.

Don't ever say that you do not know God's will. JEHOVAH ROHI lives within you, and the Bible says His Spirit will lead you into **all** truth—the truth of His perfect will. Hold fast to what the Word says.

One time, God told Elijah to speak to King Ahab. Elijah had been very concerned for Israel, because it had turned its back on the Lord and had begun to worship idols. Ahab's nasty wife, Jezebel, had led the entire nation into worshiping a certain idol named Baal.

God told Elijah, "I told My people that if they worshiped idols, I would close the heavens, and it wouldn't rain. I want you to take this message to Ahab."

Elijah took that promise to Ahab . . . but then Elijah ran away. What happened? The Word of the Lord came to him, and God took him to a little brook called Cherith, where God fed him morning and evening, supplying him with food brought by the ravens. After awhile, it was time for Elijah to move again.

God told him, "This brook is drying up from the drought, and I have plans for you to bring My people out of idolatry."

Elijah ended up in Zarapheth, where Ahab and Jezebel lived. The Word of the Lord came to him again, saying, "Tell Ahab to bring all the prophets of Baal to the top of Mount Carmel. Let them build an altar, and you rebuild the altar that has been torn down. Then let the God Who answers by fire be God. Let's settle this once and for all!"

The prophets of Baal liked the idea, because Baal was supposedly a "god of fire":

> *And they took the bullock which was given them, and they dressed it, and called on the name of Baal from morning even until noon, saying, O Baal, hear us. But there was no voice, nor any that answered. And they leaped upon the altar which was made. And it came to pass at noon, that Elijah mocked them, and said, Cry aloud: for he is a god; either he is talking, or he is pursuing, or he is in a journey, or peradventure he sleepeth, and must be awaked. And they cried aloud, and cut themselves after their manner with knives and lancets, till the blood gushed out upon them* (I Kings 18:26-28).

There was Elijah, taunting the prophets of Baal, "Your god must be on vacation. Maybe he's deaf, maybe he's taking a nap." Then, Elijah repaired the altar that had been torn down. He put a bullock on it and prayed simply:

> *. . . LORD God of Abraham, Isaac, and of Israel, let it be known this day that thou art God in Israel, and that I am thy servant, and that I have done all these things at thy word. Hear me, O LORD, hear me, that this people may know that thou art the LORD God, and that thou hast turned their heart back again. Then the fire of the LORD fell, and consumed the burnt sacrifice, and the wood, and the stones, and the dust, and licked up the water that was in the trench* (I Kings 18:36-38).

God not only consumed the sacrifice, but the wood, stones, dust, and nearby water as well. Why? Because JEHOVAH ROHI was leading and guiding Elijah, just as He desires to lead and guide you.

After this happened, the Israelites all repented before JEHOVAH God. Elijah told them to kill all of Baal's prophets, and they obeyed. Then Elijah began to pray, and the Lord opened the heavens and sent rain to end the terrible drought.

The hand of the Lord came upon Elijah, and he ran in the Lord's strength into Jezreel, before the chariot of Ahab, in that rain. When he arrived at Jezreel, bad news arrived too. Jezebel had sent Elijah a note saying that she intended to kill him, since he had killed her prophets. Instead of waiting for the Word from the Lord, Elijah ran away.

JEHOVAH ROHI had been leading Elijah by His Word, but Elijah missed it and ran from what God had for him. After running away, Elijah prayed to die, because he was so depressed about his failure. Then JEHOVAH ROHI caused Elijah to sleep and sent an angel to feed him. After Elijah ate a second time, JEHOVAH ROHI told him to go to Mount Horeb, which was forty days away. The word **horeb** means "fresh inspiration," and that is exactly what the Lord intended for Elijah. He was directing Elijah into good things.

When Elijah arrived at Mount Horeb, God taught him a lesson about trusting in JEHOVAH ROHI's guidance. Elijah walked into a cave, and suddenly, a tremendous wind rushed through. Elijah thought, "That's God!"

But God said, "No it isn't."

Then a big earthquake shook the ground. Elijah thought, "That's God!"

Again, God said, "No."

After that, God caused fire to come. Elijah thought, "That's God!"

Yet again, God said, "No." Then He said, "Elijah, **I am the still, small voice. I am the Word inside you, and that is how I will guide you. Quit looking for huge, outward manifestations. Just look to my Word inside of you.**"

The psalmist said, *"Thy word have I hid in mine heart, that I might not sin against thee"* (Psalm 119:11).

JEHOVAH was saying, "I want to lead you with My Word. When you listen to My Word, you won't sin, Elijah." Then the Lord said, "Elijah, I'm not finished with you yet. I am giving you fresh inspiration up here and showing you how to be led by the Word and not blow it. Don't worry about Ahab and Jezebel—they're going to die."

Then Elijah was instructed that a man named Elisha would be sent to take over his prophetic ministry when the Lord was ready to take Elijah home! That was fresh inspiration!

Elijah never blew it again. Why? He learned that JEHOVAH ROHI was inside him to lead and guide him. Your image in Jesus is that you're **filled with** the knowledge of His will! You do not have to wonder whether you are in God's will. He is the JEHOVAH, your Shepherd. He promised to lead you into ALL truth. What good news!

Isn't it a comfort to know the Lord as JEHOVAH ROHI? And it's great to know He desires to keep us in His perfect will. By knowing Him as your JEHOVAH ROHI, you can always be confident enough to say, "Surely goodness and mercy shall follow me all the days of my life!" When you need assurance of His guidance, there are plenty of scriptures that will beautifully direct you.

*Now the God of peace, that brought again from the dead our Lord Jesus, that great shepherd of the sheep, through the blood of the everlasting covenant, Make you perfect in every good work to do his will, working in you that which is well-pleasing in his sight, through Jesus Christ; to whom be glory for ever and ever. Amen* (Hebrews 13:20,21).

*"For ye were as sheep going astray; but are now returned unto the Shepherd and Bishop of your souls"* (I Peter 2:25).

*"And when the chief Shepherd shall appear, ye shall receive a crown of glory that fadeth not away"* (I Peter 5:4).

*I am the good shepherd, and know my sheep, and am known of mine. As the Father knoweth me, even so know I the Father: and I lay down my life for the sheep. And other sheep I have, which are not of this fold: them also I must bring, and they shall hear my voice; and there shall be one fold, and one shepherd* (John 10:14-16).

# Chapter Twelve

# JEHOVAH SHAMMAH

JEHOVAH SHAMMAH means "JEHOVAH is there." This name is first found in Ezekiel 48:35, where Ezekiel speaks of a city:

> "... *and the name of the city from that day shall be, The LORD is there*" (Ezekiel 48:35).

This is the Lord's promise and pledge to His people that His presence would be with them. Let's examine why this name was first recorded in this particular place in Ezekiel.

Ezekiel was prophesying, probably while in captivity in Babylon. At the time, Israel was falling continually into sin, and Jerusalem was about to go under. Everything was bad news!

So the Lord led Ezekiel to prophesy about a new temple, the likes of which the Lord's people had never before seen. After prophesying about this temple, Ezekiel said, **"The presence of the Lord will be there."**

The people loved Jerusalem and the temple. Now that the temple had been destroyed, they were full of sorrow and in Babylonian captivity. Reflecting upon their sorrow, they hung their harps upon willow trees and cried, "How shall we sing JEHOVAH'S song in a strange land?" We cannot sing of joy in a strange land, because we are captive. Psalms 137:5,6 shows the Israelites' love for Jerusalem:

> *If I forget thee, O Jerusalem, let my right hand forget her cunning. If I do not remember thee, let my tongue cleave to the roof of my mouth; if I prefer not Jerusalem above my chief joy.*

Ezekiel's prophecy brought his people great consolation and

hope for the restoration of their land. This was JEHOVAH'S pledge of His presence in a glorious way that they could not imagine.

However, the Israelites were obsessed with having a natural presence of God that they could perceive through their senses. But God's presence was not just an article that they could hang up in a temple. He has always wanted His presence to be so much more than that. God's presence is first recorded in the garden of Eden in Genesis 3:8:

> *"And they heard the voice of the LORD God walking in the garden in the cool of the day: . . . . "*

Why has God always desired to have His presence with His people? He desires their fellowship. God, Who had created man and placed him in a beautiful garden, came down and walked and talked with him. The presence of God was there, because He wanted man's presence with Himself. JEHOVAH SHAMMAH wants to have fellowship with you. He is present and alive in you—**He is there.**

But the presence and fellowship that existed in the garden of Eden did not last between the Lord and His people. Why? Because Adam sinned. The Word of God does not say that His presence left Adam; rather, it says that Adam left God. Adam hid behind a tree after willfully sinning. When God came to visit with him, He said, "Adam, Adam where are you?" Of course, God is all-knowing, and He knew where Adam was. God knew that Adam was hiding, because of the sin that had separated him from his Creator.

But that did not stop God from wanting fellowship with His creation. He still took every possible opportunity to continue that fellowship: He walked with Enoch, talked to Abraham and called him "friend," and communed with Moses.

One day, God spoke to Moses:

*"And let them make me a sanctuary; that I may dwell among them"* (Exodus 25:8).

At this time, God's people lived in tents and were constantly moving. Everything had to be portable, and it wasn't very beautiful or glamorous. But God said, "I want My presence to be in the tent too. If you are a pilgrim, I want to be a pilgrim with you. If you live in a tent, I will abide there with you."

God fellowships with you—wherever you are! So the presence of God came down as a pillar of cloud and a pillar of fire over the Holy of Holies, and He occupied a tent with tent dwellers.

Are you out in the "wilderness"? Do you feel like you're running around in a dry desert? Well, God was saying, "If that is where you are, that's where I want to be":

*"And there I will meet with thee, and I will commune with thee. . . "* (Exodus 25:22).

God is **there** with you, communing with you, because He is your JEHOVAH SHAMMAH.

Finally, the day came when the Israelites entered the Promised Land. It only took six and one-half years to conquer the land! The Israelites settled down with their own land, trees, crops, and homes. Later, God told King Solomon, "Build Me a temple." Since the people were now living in houses rather than tents, God desired a house too. So God dwelt in the elegant, rich Temple that was built by Solomon. There God continued to fellowship with His people. His presence was there.

First Kings 8:11 describes one of the wonderful worship services held in Solomon's temple:

*"So that the priests could not stand to minister because of the cloud: for the glory of the LORD had filled the house of the LORD."*

The presence of God Himself came in and filled up the Temple. Why? God wanted to be with His people. He wanted to abide in their praise.

But that did not last, either, because Solomon's Temple was temporary, just as the garden and the tabernacle were both temporary. So God said, "I'm going to have to deal with the people, because they have forsaken Me, although My presence has been with them. They've left Me, and they are following idols."

Ezekiel had a vision about God's presence leaving the Temple. Ezekiel saw it lift from the Holy of Holies, hover over the city's wall, and then rise into the sky—away from His people.

God's presence left the Temple. It was tragic to the people. They were carried into Babylonian captivity for 70 years where they had their fill of idolatry.

They never touched idols again after that. Still, the Lord had told them, "I'll never leave you. Although you have abandoned Me, I will never abandon you."

Just as Jeremiah had prophesied, finally after 70 years of captivity, the Israelites returned to their land of promise. It is really touching how God never gives up on us. He continually gives us opportunities to be right with Him and remain in His presence.

When the children of Israel returned to the Promised Land, they built another temple, which was called Zerubbabel's temple. It was very crude in comparison to Solomon's temple. The people were poor, and they had to scrape things together just to be able to build at all:

> *And this house was finished on the third day of the month Adar, which was in the sixth year of the reign of Darius the king. And the children of Israel, the priests, and the Levites, and the rest of the children of the captivity, kept the dedication of this house of God with joy* (Ezra 6:15,16).

The old men cried when they saw this temple and remembered the grandness of Solomon's temple. This temple could never compare to the previous temple's standards. But the young people rejoiced, because they didn't know what it was to have any other temple. They were just glad to have one!

The Bible says that the quality of this structure did not determine His presence there. His presence still rested upon it. **No matter where you are, God is there. He is JEHOVAH SHAMMAH, keeping His pledge. He will never leave nor forsake you, because His presence is within you.**

Years later, when King Herod saw Zerubbabel's temple, he thought, "How crude!" So Herod rebuilt the temple and added wealth and splendor to it. Unfortunately, Herod wanted only to build a name for himself. He hated God; therefore, God's shekinah glory did not rest upon the temple.

Jesus ministered in the outer court of this temple and called it a den of thieves. Where was God's presence at this time? The Bible says that God was in His Son, Jesus Christ. God's presence moved into the bodily temple of His son:

> *To wit, that God was in Christ, reconciling the world unto himself, not imputing their trespasses unto them; and hath committed unto us the word of reconciliation* (II Corinthians 5:19).

No wonder Jesus told the Pharisees:

> *. . . Destroy this temple, and in three days I will raise it up. Then said the Jews, Forty and six years was this temple in building, and wilt thou rear it up in three days? But he spake of the temple of his body* (John 2:19-21).

Colossians 2:9 says, *"For in him dwelleth all the fulness of the Godhead bodily."* One of Jesus' names is **Emmanuel,** meaning "God with us." God dwelt within Jesus then—and He still does now.

All the man-made temples were very short-lived: God did not stay in the garden; the tabernacle was substituted with a temple; Solomon's temple was destroyed by Nebuchadnezzar; Zerubbabel's temple was destroyed by Herod; and, finally, sinful people crucified Jesus. Now, where was the presence of God? After Jesus' resurrection, those who received Him as Savior and Lord became His temples! **You are now the temple of God.** When you invited Jesus into your heart, JEHOVAH SHAMMAH began to dwell within you:

> *"Know ye not that ye are the temple of God, and that the Spirit of God dwelleth in you?"* (I Corinthians 3:16).

> *. . . for ye are the temple of the living God; as God hath said, I will dwell in them, and walk in them; and I will be their God, and they shall be my people* (II Corinthians 6:16).

Colossians 1:27 says, "*. . . which is Christ **in** you, the hope of glory.*" You might ask, "But, Marilyn, if God dwells within my body, what will happen when I die?" Yes, your body is temporary. It will be destroyed by death, the last enemy, unless Jesus comes before that time. But the Lord has something even better in store for you after you die. He said He will always be with you:

> *For we know that if our earthly house of this tabernacle were dissolved, we have a building of God, an house not made with hands, eternal in the heavens* (II Corinthians 5:1).

God is saying, "Don't worry. I have a temple. I'll always have a place for My presence with you. But this time it is eternal, in heaven. You will be in My presence forever."

In the beginning God came down to earth to fellowship with man. But now, we have ended up with man going up to dwell with God forever. How good God is! He unfolds His beautiful plan and picture—JEHOVAH SHAMMAH.

The Bible tells us that, from the very beginning, God wanted His presence felt. He once spoke to Moses, saying, "My presence shall go with you, and I will give you rest." Moses wouldn't go anywhere if he didn't know that God's presence went with him! But you don't have to worry about that. He is **in** you!

*In all their affliction he was afflicted, and the angel of his presence saved them: in his love and in his pity he redeemed them; and he bare them, and carried them all the days of old* (Isaiah 63:9).

The Lord's presence is what has saved you. His presence is there to feel what you feel and take you through each situation. It is what you need in every moment of your life.

David loved Jehovah's presence. He even wanted to build a house for His presence, but the Lord would not allow it.

The presence of God is wonderful, and His glory goes everywhere you go. **Glory** always relates to **shekinah,** which means "to live in you."

That is why God said that He would dwell **in** you. He said, *"I will live in you, walk in you, and be your God, and you will be my people."* (See II Corinthians 6:16.)

Where does God's presence go? **It goes where you go.** When is His presence with you? **When you sleep, when you wake up, when you walk, work, or eat. No matter where you go, JEHOVAH IS THERE!**

*In whom all the building fitly framed together groweth unto an holy temple in the Lord: In whom ye also are builded together for an habitation of God through the Spirit* (Ephesians 2:21,22).

The Lord is building us, the Church, into His most glorious temple ever. We will all be one in Him, living with Him in an eternal dwelling place. No matter where we go, **He is JEHOVAH SHAMMAH!** We are just traveling through this life on earth, taking His presence to others. But we can say, just as the apostle Paul said, "My citizenship is in heaven":

> *And I saw a new heaven and a new earth: for the*
> *first heaven and the first earth were passed away;*
> *and there was no more sea. And I John saw the holy*
> *city, new Jerusalem, coming down from God out*
> *of heaven, prepared as a bride adorned for her*
> *husband. And I heard a great voice out of heaven*
> *saying, Behold, the tabernacle of God is with men,*
> *and he will dwell with them, and they shall be his*
> *people, and God himself shall be with them, and be*
> *their God* (Revelation 21:1-3).

That beautiful city has precious stone, a crystal river, delectable food, and a tree of life with leaves for the healing of the nations. It is full of Jesus' light, love, and holiness. It is full of worship, joy, and safety.

There will be no curse, adversary, defilement, nor any sorrow. Every wicked doer will be cut off, and JEHOVAH'S glory will be manifested in fullness. Together, we'll say:

> "*. . . Blessing, and honour, and glory, and power,*
> *be unto him that sitteth upon the throne and unto*
> *the Lamb for ever and ever*" (Revelation 5:13).

Why? **His eternal presence will be forever there! FOREVER we will dwell with JEHOVAH SHAMMAH!**

Not only is JEHOVAH there, however—he is **here.** He is with you and in you. He will never leave you nor forsake you—not even for a second! When you are surrounded with difficult circumstances, or when all is going well, look to His presence inside you. It's abiding within you.

Are you in a tabernacle? A wilderness? He's there. Are you in a garden? He is there. Are you in a temple? He is there. JEHOVAH is in you, walking and talking. His being is there. Don't ever forget it. When you look in the mirror, say, **"Jesus is in me, the hope of glory!"**

Wherever you go, the Lord goes with you. What a privilege it is to live in the sweet presence of the Lord each day. Study these scriptures. Realize His pledge to abide with you forever—it is His promise to complete what He has begun in your life. Truly, **JEHOVAH is there!**

*Therefore my heart is glad, and my glory rejoiceth: my flesh also shall rest in hope. Thou wilt shew me the path of life: in thy presence is fulness of joy; at thy right hand there are pleasures for evermore* (Psalm 16:9,11).

*"Know ye not that ye are the temple of God, and that the Spirit of God dwelleth in you?"* (I Corinthians 3:16).

*Go ye therefore, and teach all nations, baptizing them in the name of the Father, and of the Son, and of the Holy Ghost: Teaching them to observe all things whatsoever I have commanded you: and, lo, I am with you alway, even unto the end of the world. Amen* (Matthew 28:19,20).

*Now therefore ye are no more strangers and foreigners, but fellowcitizens with the saints, and of the household of God; And are built upon the foundation of the apostles and prophets, Jesus Christ himself being the chief corner stone; In whom all the building fitly framed together groweth unto an holy temple in the Lord: In whom ye also are builded together for an habitation of God through the Spirit* (Ephesians 2:19-22).

# Chapter Thirteen

# EL ELYON

**E**ach of us have areas in our personalities that are not complete—areas where we feel "something is just not quite right." I have these areas and you do too. God foresaw the damage that Satan and sin would produce in our lives, so He created a plan to repair our fragmented personalities. In His Word He showed us pieces and parts of His total being by using many names for Himself—each one with its own facet of meaning and ability for us.

Every name of God fits like a replacement part into a broken personality. When we incorporate these individual "parts" into the broken, hurting places in our own lives, we become whole. Like a newly overhauled car, our lives begin to run smoothly.

For instance, if you have found that you are missing power in your life, if Satan is running over you and you don't know how to hold him back, then go to the "missing parts" department of God's Word. As you study the name EL ELYON, you will discover the missing link to the mighty authority you already possess.

EL ELYON is one of the most majestic names we find in all the scriptures. It means "The God Most High," or "The Mighty One Most High," a name which carries great authority on our behalf.

EL ELYON comes from the root word *alah*, meaning "to go up, ascend, climb, exalt." It is a name that says there is no existing thing—no god—that is higher than the Most High God. He is the possessor of heaven, earth, and everything in them. His name is so high, so exalted, so marvelous, that there is no other name to compare with this name. EL ELYON is a name that is untouchable in quality, and incomprehensible in dominion and might.

This name is so majestic that EL ELYON was the name

above all names that Satan coveted most for himself. Isaiah says that Satan spoke in his heart:

> *. . . I will ascend to heaven; I will raise my throne above the stars of God, and I will sit on the mount of assembly in the recesses of the north. I will ascend above the heights of the clouds; I will make myself like the Most High (EL ELYON)* (Isaiah 14:13,14 NAS).

If you remember, the root word for EL ELYON means "to ascend, go up, climb." Notice in this verse that Satan says "I will ascend; I will go up." He makes five **I will** statements. **Five** times in **five** different ways he says, "I will take the place of EL ELYON, the Most High God." But EL ELYON turns around in the next verses and gives **five** "you will" declarations to show that He is truly the "Most" High God!

In verses 15 through 20 God says, "Satan, **you will** be thrown into hell, **you will** be gazed upon, **you will** be talked about, **you will** be cast out of your grave like a carcass, and **you will** be alone."

The Most High had the last Word for Satan then, and He still does now! Anytime Satan exalts himself above the knowledge of God in your life, bring EL ELYON on to the scene. The Mighty Most High God will always have the last Word for anyone who chooses to challenge His authority.

As an example, let's look at the Old Testament prophet, Balaam. The Bible says of him:

> *He hath said, which heard the words of God, and knew the knowledge of the most High, which saw*

199

> *the vision of the Almighty, falling into a trance, but*
> *having his eyes open* (Numbers 24:16).

Balaam had "the knowledge of the most High" (EL ELYON). He knew God and had even experienced open visions from God, but being caught up in visions from the Most High was not as important to Balaam as being "caught up" with the love of money.

The king of Moab had bribed Balaam to use his power to curse the Israelites. He said, "Balaam, if you go back to your old life and curse the Israelites, I'll give you lots of money, and I'll give you a high position—I'll **exalt** you!"

Balaam tried to twist God's arm and get His permission to do this. But God refused, so Balaam tried anyway.

Balaam went up on a mountain to curse Israel, but when he got up there, the only things that would come out of his mouth were blessings! This greatly displeased the King of Moab, so Balaam remarked, "Let's try another mountain. Maybe we're looking at this thing in the wrong direction."

They ascended another mountain and the same thing happened. This time the disgruntled Moab king said, "I'm disgusted with you. I am paying you to help me defeat my enemy, but all you're doing is blessing them."

Balaam thought to himself, "Well the north and south didn't work," so he headed east and tried cursing the Israelites there, but again to no avail.

The furious Moabite king convinced him to try cursing one more time in the west. However, on the fourth attempt, Balaam **blessed** the Israelites more than ever!

That is good news! No one can curse what God has blessed! Whether a curse comes from the north, the south, the east, or the west makes no difference, because the Most High is above all evil. EL ELYON is higher than all our circumstances; He always has the last Word, and the last Word is always "victory!"

We see this victory principle when the name EL ELYON is introduced in Genesis for the first time:

> *And Melchizedek king of Salem brought forth bread and wine: and he was the priest of the most high God. And he blessed him, and said, Blessed be Abram of the most high God, possessor of heaven and earth: And blessed be the most high God, which hath delivered thine enemies into thy hand. And he gave him tithes of all. And the king of Sodom said unto Abram, Give me the persons, and take the goods to thyself. And Abram said to the king of Sodom, I have lift up mine hand unto the LORD, the most high God, the possessor of heaven and earth* (Genesis 14:18-22).

In this episode, Abraham had just conquered **four** armies with a little over one-hundred men. Now that's victory! Something has to be working for you when you can do that! EL ELYON had brought Abraham to a decisive victory which produced great wealth and possessions for "the father of many nations."

Abraham acknowledged his new-found revelation that God was EL ELYON—The Most High God—the God who lifts His children higher than any problem they can ever encounter. He is the God who is higher than our lack, higher than our diseases, and even higher than our nasty in-laws! The ability of His name is greater than any other name in existence.

This ability of the Most High God is incorporated into our lives in four ways. These are the four "p's" to authority.

Daniel is my favorite example of one who used the "four p's principle" to move high above his circumstances. This young man knew how to trust the Most High above extraordinary dilemmas.

First of all, he was separated from his family. When he arrived in Babylon, he was made a eunuch, which means he was altered physically. He could not marry nor be a father. He was a slave in a place where he had to eat food that he felt was unholy and ungodly.

In spite of all these adverse circumstances, Daniel **purposed** in his heart that he would serve the Most High God no matter what. This is the first "p."

He **purposed** in his heart that not only was God the Most High God, but that He would be the most high in his life. So very wisely Daniel and two of his buddies approached the eunuch in charge of him, and proposed a test.

He said, "I believe there is a healthier way to eat. Will you let us eat according to the laws of the Most High, and see if we look better than the rest?"

If you remember, at the end of ten days they were fatter and healthier than all the others, and they had great favor with the man in charge, as well.

He **purposed** to trust the Most High, and the Most High lifted Daniel higher than his circumstances. So never say, "I'm fine under the circumstances." What are you doing **under** them? Let the Most High put you on *top* of them!

Once Daniel **purposed** in his heart, something else began to happen. During this time the king had a dream, but he couldn't remember it. In frustration he called his wise men and demanded they tell him his dream and its interpretation.

The wise men protested, "Hey, King, you can't ask us to do this! No one could perform something that unreasonable."

So the king threw a tantrum, "What good are wise men then? I'll just kill you all."

Now Daniel heard what had happened, so he moved into action—he **prayed**. Daniel and his friends held an all-night prayer meeting where he got the dream and the interpretation.

Notice that out of the second "p," came the third "p"—**perception.**

There is one path to climb to the heights of spiritual perception, and that path is called **prayer.**

So Daniel took his revelation to the king and said, "Now I didn't get this revelation by myself—no one could do that. But the MOST HIGH GOD gave me the revelation and the interpretation." Then Daniel went on to relate the dream and its meaning.

King Nebuchadnezzar was so astonished that he fell upon his face and worshiped! The king caught a glimpse of EL ELYON, the Most High:

> *The king answered unto Daniel, and said, Of a truth it is, that your God is a God of gods, and a Lord of kings, and a revealer of secrets, seeing thou couldest reveal this secret. Then the king made Daniel a great man, and gave him many great gifts, and made him ruler over the whole province . . .* (Daniel 2:47-48).

Daniel ended up with the fourth "p"—**power!** Notice we don't start with **power**, we start with **purpose** and **prayer**, then we move to **perception** and **power**.

The difference between Daniel and Nebuchadnezzar was that even though the Most High had revealed himself to both of them, Nebuchadnezzar had not **purposed** in his heart to make EL ELYON **his** Most High God and soon forgot about Him. Rather, he had grown quite fond of himself and decided everyone else should feel likewise!

He made an image of himself and demanded that everyone worship the image, an area that the Mighty Most High will not tolerate, because all worship belongs to Him and Him alone. So in response, God gives Nebuchadnezzar another dream which Daniel is called upon to interpret:

> *This is the interpretation, O king, and this is the decree of the most High (EL ELYON), which is come upon my lord the king: That they shall drive thee from men, and thy dwelling shall be with the beasts of the field, and they shall make thee to eat grass as oxen, and they shall wet thee with the dew of heaven, and seven times shall pass over thee, till thou know that the most High (EL ELYON) ruleth in the kingdom of men, and giveth it to whomsoever he will* (Daniel 4:24-25).

Daniel told the king, "You have an outstanding kingdom here, Nebuchadnezzar, but if you don't give God credit for it, you're going to lose your mind. For seven years you'll think you are an animal. Only when you give glory to EL ELYON, the Most High God, will your sanity return. All you have to do is repent and make Him the Most High of your life, and this terrible thing will never happen."

A year had passed, but Nebuchadnezzar had still not heeded the warning. Then one day the king walked out on his balcony, and he looked at the hanging gardens that he had build for his wife. (He had built them because his wife was homesick for the mountains where she was raised. The hanging gardens were so beautiful that they were one of the seven wonders of the ancient world.)

So Nebuchadnezzar looked out at the beautiful big mountain that he had built, and thought to himself, "I built that. I built the greatest empire the world has ever known. I'm wonderful, aren't I?"

That was the wrong thing to think! If you want to be the most high, you have to become the most low. You have to humble yourself in the presence of God.

Nebuchadnezzar went stark raving mad and barked like a dog.

Can you imagine somebody driving in to see the king? They would pass the beautiful hanging gardens, gawking at the flowers, when some funny looking little face with long hair would come peeking through the shrubs and go, "Bark, bark, bark, bark!"

"Who's that!" they'd inquire.

"Oh, it's just the king."

"The king?"

"Yea, he went crazy, because he thought he built this empire without God, and God brought him down."

God is **always** going to be the Most High. No one challenges that position and comes out winning.

Finally, after seven years, Nebuchadnezzar got tired of barking, and Daniel 4:34 tells us that one day he raised up his eyes to heaven to the Most High. When he did, his understanding returned, and he blessed EL ELYON.

After that his kingdom continued to flourish.

Like Nebuchadnezzar, we sometimes get an exalted opinion of ourselves—at least I have.

One time when I had just started to travel, I went to preach for a pastor. I wanted to be polite, so I asked him, "How long shall I preach."

He answered abruptly, "As long as you're anointed. When you're not anointed, I want you to sit down. And if you don't sit down, I'll make you sit down!"

My dignity was extremely offended. I thought, "Thanks a lot. I'll just preach some place else."

But God dealt with me about my self-exalted attitude, and now this pastor is one of the dearest friends I have.

If I had stayed in my ego bubble very long, God would have had to deal with me and burst the bubble, just like he "burst the bubble" of Nebuchadnezzar's grandson, Belshazzar.

Belshazzar was a real smart-aleck kid. His father was out on a military campaign, and he decides to have a big party—a drunken brawl. Everybody was drunk, and the party was getting a little dull, so he said, "Let's do something exciting!"

Belshazzar orders the golden vessels from the temple in Jerusalem to be brought to the party. They began to degrade the holy vessels, drinking from them while they praised the gods of gold and silver. In reality, they were defying the Most High God.

In that hour, the hand of God appears on the scene and begins writing on the wall. If screeching nails on a chalkboard makes you squeemish, think what God's hand, writing on a nearby wall would do to you! It actually caused the first knee knocking to be recorded in the Bible! Scripture records that

Belhazzar's knees began to smite "one against another." He was drunk, but I'd say he had a **sobering** experience!

So the petrified king screamed at the top of his lungs, "Get somebody in here quick!"

Daniel was brought in to interpret the meaning of the message, "Mene, Mene, Tekel, Upharsin," which was written upon the wall.

Daniel looked at it and said, "Listen, Belshazzar, your grandfather found the Most High God, and you'd better get with it. If you don't repent and make Him the Most High of your life, your kingdom is going to be divided tonight, and given to the Medes and the Persians. You're going to be killed."

Unfortunately, Belshazzar did not repent. For refusing to submit to the Most High, he became the most low. He lost the kingdom and was killed that very night. Once again the Most High had the last word for those who challenged Him, and exalted themselves above Him—giving us one more example of God's ability to establish and maintain His great authority as the Most High over our circumstances.

He showed me the reality of that one time when we were planning our first women's convention. I had no idea how many people would come, so I determined that 2,000 women would be just the right amount to hold the convention in our church. I thought my goal was a pretty high number for the Most High God. That is all the faith I had.

The registrations were coming into the office and my staff kept telling me how all these people were registered. They would say, "Marilyn, where are we going to put all these people?"

I had already decided 2,000, so I made no provision in my faith for the Most High God. But the day before the convention my staff came to me and said, "Marilyn, please listen to us. We have 2,500 reservations, and that doesn't count the people who are coming without reservations! Marilyn, most of these people are from out of town. What are we going to do about all the local people?"

At first I said to myself, "They registered, but they won't all come." But I went home and started thinking about it. What if everybody does show? What if a lot of people show that didn't even register? Oh! What about all the local people?

Then I remembered that EL ELYON was higher than the highest number of women that would show up at that convention. I could have panicked, but instead, I presented my predicament to the Most High, "God, what are **You** going to do?"

He spoke to me and said, "I know how to take care of crowds—look what I did in the wilderness. I fed two million people when they got tired of manna. They wanted meat so I sent the quail by way of the wind, and I am going to send the wind of the Holy Spirit and blow in a provision for you."

Do you know what He did? He blew a coliseum to us that afternoon!

When I got to the coliseum and saw all those people, the Lord spoke to me and said, "You know, Marilyn, if you would have seen Me as the Most High God, I would have brought ten thousand people here; but you were so busy with two . . . !"

I want to tell you that God is bigger than anything we face. When we look at the nations and what is going on around us, God is bigger. God is bigger than war, bigger than Khadafy, even bigger than terrorists.

One famous terrorist in history was a giant named Goliath who defied the Most High God. He boasted, "I'm a big man around here," but he found that God was bigger.

God humiliated big Goliath by using little David—a simple shepherd boy who knew that the Most High was taller than nine-foot giants. Not only is the Most High taller than giants, He is bigger than kings.

King Saul tried to kill David for nine years, with 21 attempts on David's life; but the Most High protected him. Through his trials David learned to know the Most High in a personal relationship, recording the Psalms out of these intimate experiences. It is in Psalms that we find the most diversified overview of what this name will do for us.

Psalms 18:13-17 reveals EL ELYON as our **voice of victory.**

Psalms 21:7 says that our **security and stability** rests in the Most High.

Psalms 57:2 states He **performs and accomplishes** all things on our behalf.

Psalms 78:35 reveals that EL ELYON and Jesus are one and the same, for in this passage, the Most High God is called **redeemer.**

Psalms 82:6 calls us the **children** of the Most High God.

Psalms 91:1-9 promises that He is our secret shelter and abiding place:

> *He that dwelleth in the secret place of THE MOST HIGH shall abide under the shadow of the Almighty .... Because thou hast made the LORD, which is my refuge, even THE MOST HIGH, thy habitation.*

At first, the mighty God whose name is high and lifted up— EL ELYON— seems unapproachable—too high and distant for the common mortal. And true, He is high and above all other names; but as Psalm 91 indicates, He lifts us up with Him and desires us to **live** and to be our "habitation." But how do we become lifted up to Him? Let's see how Jesus did it:

> *Let this mind be in you, which was also in Christ Jesus: Who, being in the form of God, thought it not robbery to be equal with God: But made himself of no reputation, and took upon him the form of a servant, and was made in the likeness of men: And being found in fashion as a man, he humbled himself, and became obedient unto death, even the death of the cross. Wherefore God also hath highly exalted him, and given him a* **name which is above every name** (Philippians 2:5-9).

This says that Jesus was originally **equal** with EL ELYON; He had the status and supremacy of the Most High, but He chose to become the most low. He humbled Himself as a servant and died in our place, resulting in one of the most dramatic, exciting moments in the Bible.

Imagine the scene that took place after Jesus' third day in hell. The Bible tells us that Jesus stripped off Satan's armor and crushed his head. That means that Jesus removed all authority and power from Satan. Then the earth began to tremble as Jesus came forth the victor, but God didn't stop there. Because Jesus was obedient, God exalted Him and gave Him the name which Satan attempted to usurp for himself in millenniums past. Jesus' triumph is crowned with the name "which is **above** every name." He is given the name EL ELYON, the Most High God!

The next thing God did was to seat Jesus at His own right

210

hand in the Heavenly places **far** above (remember the meaning of El Elyon?) all principality and power, far above evil, far above every circumstance that has a name. Then comes the good news for us personally:

> *"And hath put all things under his feet, and gave him to be the head over all things to the church,* **Which is his body,** . . . " (Ephesians 1:22-23).

Now that we are His Body, we are seated **far** above every name that is named in this world! Even the least member in the Body of Christ—the feet—are far above every demon power and evil circumstance in existence. Ephesians 2:6 confirms this fact:

> *"And hath raised us up together, and made us sit together in heavenly places in Christ Jesus."*

One woman was set free from depression through this scripture. She said, "Depression is a name. I am seated with Christ in the heavenly places far above depression."

She started meditating and seeing herself sitting with Christ and looking down at everything that was far beneath her feet. If depression attacked, she would take her authority through Christ, stomp her foot on depression and say, "Depression, you're under my feet! You don't have any authority over me!"

I have seen hundreds and hundreds of men and women delivered from smoking in the same way. **We have been given great authority through Jesus.** We have been raised to high places in Christ, and according to Psalms we are even higher than the angels in heaven! What a privileged position of authority we have been given!

Do you have a name that needs to be put under your feet? Meditate and see yourself seated with Christ at the right hand of the Mighty Most High. Put the name of depression under your feet and stomp on it. Put the names of poverty, lack, divorce, strife, anger, disease, habit, or the name of any other afflicting circumstance under your feet and tromp them down.

You have the name of EL ELYON to back up your authority and hold you higher than anything that will ever come your way!

We have only just begun to learn the authority we have in Jesus' name, but in the next few pages you are about to discover another name that will add great strength to that authority you already possess.

## EL ELYON

*And Melchizedek king of Salem brought forth bread and wine: and he was the priest of the most **high** God. And he blessed him, and said, Blessed be Abram of the most **high** God, possessor of heaven and earth: And blessed be the most **high** God, which hath delivered thine enemies into thy hand. And he gave him tithes of all. And the king of Sodom said unto Abram, Give me the persons, and take the goods to thyself. And Abram said to the king of Sodom, I have lift up mine hand unto the LORD, the most **high** God, the possessor of heaven and earth* (Genesis 14:18-22).

*"I will praise the LORD according to his righteousness: and will sing praise to the name of the LORD most **high**"* (Psalms 7:17).

*"For the LORD most **high** is terrible; he is a great King over all the earth"* (Psalms 47:2).

*"I will cry unto God most **high**; unto God that performeth all things for me"* (Psalms 57:2).

*"Yet they tempted and provoked the most **high** God, and kept not his testimonies"* (Psalms 78:56).

*"That men may know that thou, whose name alone is JEHOVAH, art the most **high** over all the earth"* (Psalms 83:18).

*"I will ascend above the heights of the clouds; I will be like the most **High**"* (Isaiah 14:14).

*This matter is by the decree of the watchers, and the demand by the word of the holy ones: to the intent that the living may know that the most **High** ruleth in the kingdom of men, and giveth it to whomsoever he will, and setteth up over it the basest of men* (Daniel 4:17).

# Chapter Fourteen

# JEHOVAH TSEBAOTH

**D**uring the Vietnam War, the "Green Berets" became well-known as a special fighting force, carefully chosen for hand-to-hand combat. These men were publicly portrayed as being the cream of the crop within the status of military ground forces. They were the "elite of the elite," well versed in combat skills, and wore a green beret—the "crown" of ability that set them apart from other soldiers.

When we become intimately acquainted with JEHOVAH TSEBAOTH, the Lord of Hosts, we will see that we have a similar distinction. We have an elite quality—a unique position that sets us off from the rest of the world—and a crown of righteousness is our medallion of distinguishment.

According to God's Word, we are not mere men led by our five senses. We have been appointed to walk in the realm of the Spirit where we hold the status and rank of a member in the army of the Lord—JEHOVAH TSEBAOTH—the Lord of Hosts.

**Tsebaoth** comes from the Hebrew root word **tsaba,** which can be used as either a verb or a noun.

In verb form **tsaba** means "to wage war," but it also holds a broader sense of meaning: "to render service to God." This is a service of total dedication and careful regimentation associated with spiritual warfare and worship.

The noun form of **tsaba** means "armies, hosts, or multitudes." This word expresses myriads—a vast sea of varying ranks and individuals under God's command.

The Bible designates these "hosts" in categories, ranks, or echelons. The very first designation of the word "host" is not at all what you might expect because it is referring to the stars:

> *"Thus the heavens and the earth were finished, and all the host of them"* (Genesis 2:1).

Psalm 147:4 tells us that God is Lord of all the stars that He made, and He calls them by name. He even knows how many stars there are, and these stars move at His bidding to do His will—the original "Star Trek" series!

JEHOVAH TSEBAOTH invented the idea of moving stars, and the first recorded "Star Trek" adventure occurred in Judges 4 when King Jabin, an enemy of God's people, was oppressing and attacking Israel through the leadership of Sisera.

General Sisera was a military genius, who commanded 900 iron chariots—a mighty army for his day. Historically, iron chariots had wheels with vicious spikes that could literally shred an opponent into ribbons. Therefore, any army that had iron chariots was automatically the victor over any other army of that time period.

But Sisera failed to consider the God of a female judge named Deborah—the only female judge mentioned in the Bible. Deborah had a revelation of JEHOVAH TSEBAOTH. She knew that the Lord of hosts would call upon whatever host— even the heavenly host, the stars—that was necessary to fight for His people.

So JEHOVAH TSEBAOTH said to Deborah, "Go get your general, Barak, and tell him to fight against Sisera. If necessary, I will move the stars in the heavens to give you a victory."

Barak didn't have a single iron chariot to his name. He didn't even have a big army. All he had was a woman telling him, "You can do it!"

"Sure, Deborah," Barak responded, "since *you* have the revelation, and *you* have the faith in the Lord, then *you* go with me to battle!"

Deborah was a bold woman with great confidence in the Lord

217

of Hosts, so she went with Barak to Mount Tabor in Kedesh to fight Sisera. There they stood—Barak, Deborah, and their "little tag-along army" that was not too swift, certainly not well trained, and, above all, without iron chariots.

Across the valley, on the opposite mountain, Sisera and his 900 chariots roared to a stop to observe Deborah and Barak's pathetic little army. Sisera probably thought, "What's that dumb, flaky woman doing up there? And look at that little silly army—let's have a fifteen-minute battle and show them who's boss!"

Then Sisera commanded his men to descend into the valley because that was where the two armies would meet to fight. Strategically, the valley was a good battleground for Sisera's chariots. The river bed in the valley was completely dry from lack of rain, so there were no natural barriers to deter his attack.

As Sisera's chariots thundered down into the valley, Barak and his meager band charged down with their little clubs and stones in hand. They had placed their trust entirely in JEHOVAH TSEBAOTH. But that was the best thing they could have done because, suddenly, it started to rain, and a deluge of water cascaded from the sky.

Have you ever tried to drive an iron chariot through the mud? Sisera did, but those iron wheels just got bogged down in the mud . . . and Sisera was so frightened that he jumped out of his foundering chariot and ran from the battle. Unquestionably, Barak won the victory.

What had happened? In Judges 5, Deborah sang a poetic revelation of that event. She sang about how God moved the stars in the heavens. When the stars started to move, the weather was affected; and, as a result, the rain began to fall.

218

Just as God moved His hosts of stars on behalf of the entire nation of Israel, He would also command His hosts for the sake of one individual. As King Hezekiah lay on his death bed, the prophet Isaiah prophesied to him:

> " . . . *Thus saith the LORD, 'Set thine house in order; for thou shalt die, and not live'"* (II Kings 20:1).

Then Isaiah turned and walked out the door.

But Hezekiah wasn't ready to die. He didn't have a child to inherit the throne, and he desired to have a son before he died. So he "turned his face to the wall" and began to pray:

> " . . . *'remember now how I have walked before thee in truth and with a perfect heart, and have done that which is good in thy sight' . . . "* (II Kings 20:3).

Isaiah was just walking out of the king's palace when God spoke to him, "Isaiah, go back and tell Hezekiah that I have heard his prayer. I will add 15 years to his life."

When Isaiah returned to tell Hezekiah, the king said, "You told me I was going to die, so how do I know I will live?"

Isaiah replied, "You name it. God will do it."

Hezekiah thought for awhile and replied, "It wouldn't be very hard for JEHOVAH TSEBAOTH to make the sun stand still; so instead, tell God to make the sun—the star of the solar system—to go backward."

> *And Isaiah the prophet cried unto the LORD: and he brought the shadow ten degrees backward, by which it had gone down in the dial of Ahaz* (II Kings 20:11).

God did as Hezekiah had requested! God is in command of the sun, the moon, and the stars. He commands those hosts, because He is the Lord of Hosts.

Upon another occasion, Joshua was out fighting to take the Promised Land for his people. A terrible conflict had been waged, and Joshua knew in his heart that he would lose the battle if he didn't finish it before sunset. So Joshua, knowing the Lord of Hosts, cried out, " . . . *Sun, stand thou still upon Gibeon; and thou, Moon, in the valley of Ajalon*" (Joshua 10:12). **It worked!** The Lord answered Joshua's prayer, and he won the battle!

How did he have the courage to pray like that? Because Joshua had a revelation of the authority and elite quality he possessed in JEHOVAH TSEBAOTH, the Lord of the Hosts of stars.

The Lord manifested Himself as JEHOVAH TSEBAOTH to me the first time I went to Ethiopia. Forty-two people, including Paul Cole (my cameraman) and myself, were waiting to be transported by Russian helicopter into the most drought-stricken area of Ethiopia.

The first problem we encountered was that the helicopter only held twenty-one people. So the communists said to me, "Marilyn, you and your cameraman go first, because it's 4:30 in the afternoon, and it looks like it might rain. You need to get your video pictures, so you go first while it is still light."

This was evidence of God's favor because the other people who were waiting included several American congressmen and their aides. The communists certainly wanted to make a good impression on the congressmen, because the results of their investigation would determine the amount of financial aid given to Ethiopia. However, the communists told me, "You go first."

Paul and I climbed onto the helicopter, and the head of the congressional delegation asked, "Why are you on this helicopter?"

"The communists told us to get on," I answered.

"Well, you and your cameraman have to get off," he said. "I need to get all my aides on board, so you'll just have to go with the next group."

This congressman knew it would be almost an hour before the helicopter could transport his group and return for ours, but what could I do? Paul and I got off the helicopter!

As I stepped out the communists said, "What are you doing? Why are you getting off when we told you to get on."

I was feeling a little sheepish, but I replied, "The head of the congressional delegation told us to get off."

"Well, it's our helicopter!" they said. "Now get back on!"

When I reboarded, the only seat left was next to the same congressman, who, by now, was quite irritated: "How dare you get back on this helicopter!" he snarled. "I told you to get off!"

This was one of those awful times when I felt absolutely ridiculous, but I smiled through gritted teeth and responded, "The communists told me that it's their helicopter, and we are supposed to go now."

"I don't care whose helicopter it is!" he exploded. "I need my aides, so GET OFF!"

Guess what we did? We got off! By this time Paul was about ready to cry. "Marilyn," he said, "we'll never get those pictures. We've had so many miracles and have gone through such a hassle to get this far." Suddenly tears betrayed his outward composure, "Now, we'll never get the pictures."

I put my hand on his shoulder, looked directly into his eyes, and said, "Now listen, Paul, even if we have to tell the sun to stand still, we are going to get the pictures. Don't cry—don't cry." Forty minutes later the helicopter returned for us.

Upon arriving at our destination, we disembarked from the helicopter—only to find an angry crowd of congressmen. The expressions on their faces almost startled me.

"What's wrong?" I asked.

"Well," one congressional aide grumbled, "it's been raining, and we haven't been able to see anything."

But just as the aide finished speaking, the clouds dissipated, and the sun shone brighter than ever! Best of all, our videos were outstanding! Once again, the Lord of the hosts of stars, JEHOVAH TSEBOATH, received the glory and the victory!

How exciting it is to know that as children of JEHOVAH TSEBAOTH we will not be hindered by rain, wind, or the weather! If necessary, the sun and the moon will stand still until we win the battle. But God says we are never alone in battle, because He has created another rank of hosts—the angelic hosts—who fight for us:

> *"The chariots of God are twenty thousand, even thousands of angels: the Lord is among them, as in Sinai, in the holy place"* (Psalms 68:17).

> *"Bless ye the LORD, all ye his hosts; ye ministers of his, that do his pleasure"* (Psalms 103:21).

God has a mighty and elite fighting force in the heavens that is perpetually ready to move at His command. Jesus said that if He so chose, He could pray to His heavenly Father and 12 legions of angels (that's 72,000 angels!) would instantly be at Jesus' side to deliver Him from the Cross. But Jesus said, "That's not My Father's will—I am to go by way of death. Yes, these angels would deliver Me from the Cross, but I willingly **choose** to do my Father's will."

Like Jesus, we have been given the right to call upon the hosts of heaven when we need them:

> *"Are they not all ministering spirits, sent forth to*
> *minister for them who shall be heirs of salvation?"*
> (Hebrews 1:14).

We can request of the Father, "In the name of Jesus, I call the angels from the north, the south, the east, and the west." Maybe you are in the north and you just need to call in a few angels from the north. On the other hand, maybe you need them all! In either case, you have every right to call upon Jesus, your JEHOVAH TSEBAOTH, to send His angels from every direction to minister on your behalf.

This is what Hezekiah did when he came under attack by Sennacherib. In contrast to his father Ahaz, Hezekiah was a good king who proved to be the most faithful to God of all the kings since David's time:

> *"He trusted in the LORD God of Israel; so that after*
> *him was none like him among all the kings of Judah,*
> *nor any that were before him"* (II Kings 18:5).

At the very beginning of his reign, Hezekiah began a zealous attempt to stamp out idolatry among the Israelites. He repaired the Temple and reinstated the observance of Mosaic Law.

However, the powerful Assyrian King Sennacherib invaded Judah and captured over 200,000 people. King Hezekiah attempted to buy off Sennacherib:

223

*And Hezekiah king of Judah sent to the king of Assyria to Lachish, saying, I have offended; return from me: that which thou puttest on me will I bear. And the king of Assyria appointed unto Hezekiah the king of Judah three hundred talents of silver and thirty talents of gold* (II Kings 18:14).

But this did not satisfy Sennacherib; he immediately broke his promise and prepared to attack Jerusalem. Through his general Rabshakeh, Sennacherib delivered a threatening message to Hezekiah. When he received no reply, Sennacherib sent a personal letter in which he demanded Hezekiah's complete surrender.

Hezekiah went to the Temple and prayed fervently that God would deliver Jerusalem from Sennacherib. The prophet Isaiah received a message from God assuring Hezekiah that God would defend Jerusalem. That very night "... *the angel of the Lord ... smote in the camp of the Assyrians an hundred fourscore and five thousand*" (II Kings 19:35).

When Sennacherib crawled out of bed the next morning, he marveled at how quiet the camp seemed, "Those lazy men have overslept again!" But he quickly discovered that 185,000 of his men were dead. It took just *one angel* to kill 185,00 men!

Like Hezekiah, **we** have hosts of angels to minister for us! Don't let those hosts of angels sit around all day eating manna—put them to work! I put my angels to work every morning. I picture angels surrounding my husband, children, and grandchildren. I pray that God will encompass Happy Church and Marilyn Hickey Ministries with angels who will keep us in all our ways.

As I pray, I visualize those angels. I visualize them around my daughter's little car: I see them sitting on the fender and on the bumper. I even visualize angels holding onto the door handles!

You may think, "Oh, Marilyn, that's ridiculous." But, really! That's how I see them!

When I travel, I visualize angels covering the airplane. I picture them on the wings, the tail, and with the pilot. Some angels go before me, and some go after me.

If fear tries to grip me when I am at home alone, I visualize angels around our house. I see them at the back and front doors and at every window. One angel even protects the dog and another the garage door! And I have complete peace and confidence that my angels are working.

Yes, we are protected by an elite angelic force. The Bible says that the angel of the Lord **encamps** around those who fear God (Psalms 34:7). Do **you** fear God? Do you regard Him with deep love, respect, and awe? Then you have an angelic encampment around you.

Daniel proved the truth of Psalms 34:7 when he was thrown into the lions' den. All his life Daniel had worshiped God. Daniel is one of the few well-known Bible characters about whom nothing negative is written. His life was characterized by faith, prayer, and courage. Even at 80 years of age his enemies couldn't fault him, so they chose to attack him through his religion. When he refused to comply with the decree to stop praying, Daniel was thrown into the lions' den.

When God saw what was happening, He said, "I am going to send My personal angel to protect Daniel."

So God's personal angel crept into the lions' den, leaned over, and whispered into a lion's ear, "Buster, if you even sniff at him, you're dead on the spot!"

This angel stayed with Daniel all night while lions with "lockjaw" stalked around the den. If they came near Daniel, the angel would say, "Quit that sniffing and get away from here."

Early the next morning, the king went to the lions' den and cried to Daniel:

> " . . . 'O Daniel, servant of the living God, is thy God, whom thou servest continually, able to deliver thee from the lions?'" (Daniel 6:20).

And Daniel responded:

> *"My God hath sent his angel, and hath shut the lions' mouths, . . . "* (Daniel 6:22).

The king, who truly loved Daniel, rejoiced to find him alive and commanded that he be removed from the lions' den. Then the king commanded that those who had accused Daniel be cast into the den themselves:

> *. . . and they cast them into the den of lions, them, their children, and their wives; and the lions had the mastery of them, and brake all their bones in pieces or ever they came at the bottom of the den* (Daniel 6:24).

Why did God protect Daniel and not the others who were thrown into the lions' den? Because Daniel respected and loved God. The others mocked Him and, therefore, removed themselves from His divine protection.

The Lord of the angelic hosts never sleeps, and His angelic hosts are instantly obedient to His Word. For example, there is a hilarious situation in II Kings 6 concerning Elisha and some Syrians. These Syrians operated under a terrorist-type spirit and used guerrilla warfare against Israel.

The Syrian "guerrillas" would try to attack Israel, but before they could carry out their plans, Elisha would receive a word from God. Therefore, Elisha always knew the Syrian tactics before they were accomplished!

Elisha would warn his king, "Don't go to such and such a place, because the terrorists from Syria plan to attack you there." And, time and time again, the king would do as Elisha said.

Eventually, the King of Syria became suspicious of men in his own army. "Who is the rat telling on us?" he asked. "Who is this traitor?"

"Nobody, sir," the servant answered. "Everybody is loyal to you here, but this prophet Elisha knows everything you whisper in your bedroom. He knows every battle plan you conceive, and he tells Israel's king." (See II Kings 6:12.)

The Syrian king didn't know about JEHOVAH TSEBAOTH, so, one night, he sent his whole band of guerrillas to surround the little town of Dothan where Elisha lived.

When Elisha's servant awakened the next morning, he scarcely believed what he saw: the whole Syrian army was surrounding Dothan! The servant ran to Elisha and screamed, "Help! We're dead—the Syrian guerrillas are here to rip us apart!"

But Elisha calmly prayed, "God, open my servant's eyes to see the mighty army of angels surrounding the terrorists."

Elisha didn't ask for his own eyes to be opened. Why?

Because he was walking by faith and not by sight. We don't need to **see angels**—we have the revelation of the Word. Once we have **seen,** we are no longer in the faith realm; we have moved into the sensory realm where Elisha's servant was.

When God opened the servant's eyes, the servant saw with his natural sight that which Elisha already knew in his spirit. The Syrians were surrounded by hosts of warring angels, who were ready for God's command.

Next Elisha asked JEHOVAH TSEBAOTH to blind the Syrians' eyes:

> *" . . . 'Smite this people, I pray thee, with blindness.'*
> *And he smote them with blindness according to the*
> *word of Elisha"* (II Kings 6:18).

I believe God assigned one angel to each Syrian enemy, and the whole host of angels put their hands over the eyes of a host of Syrian soldiers! Then single-handedly, Elisha took the entire blinded army captive—all because he had put his trust in the Lord of Hosts, Who has more than enough angels to cover the eyes of the largest armies of the world!

God can send armies of angels to surround our nation—the White House, our cities, and our churches. I believe there are even angels patrolling the air—flying overhead to guard and protect us.

That's not all! The Bible speaks of another group of "flying" hosts—the feathered hosts—who are numbered in the ranks of JEHOVAH TSEBAOTH. These feathered hosts ministered to Elijah during a critical time when he was hiding from King Ahab.

Ahab was one of the most wicked kings in the Old Testament:

> *"... and Ahab did more to provoke the LORD God of Israel to anger than all the kings of Israel that were before him"* (I Kings 16:33).

Under the influence of his wife Jezebel, Ahab had introduced Baalism to the Northern Kingdom and sanctioned it as the state's religion.

A drought and famine were sent by God to discipline the people for their idolatry:

> *And Elijah the Tishbite, who was of the inhabitants of Gilead, said unto Ahab, As the LORD God of Israel liveth, before whom I stand, there shall not be dew nor rain these years, but according to my word* (I Kings 17:1).

Ahab and Jezebel hated Elijah for the righteous stand he had taken and blamed him for the terrible famine that was progressing. So they plotted to kill him.

Elijah became a fugitive with nowhere to go. But God said, "Don't worry about a thing; you just come down here by the only brook in the land that has running water—brook Cherith. There My feathered hosts will take care of you during the next three-and-a-half years of drought."

So the Lord of the feathered hosts commanded ravens to bring bread and meat twice a day to Elijah.

Remember, this was a famine time. Normally, if a bird found a piece of meat or bread, the food would do a quick disappearing act down the bird's gullet! But these ravens didn't eat the meat or the bread—they brought it to Elijah faithfully during the time he was hiding by the brook.

God is the Lord of the feathered hosts, and these birds will carry out the plan and perfect will of God. Even now God is preparing birds for the last days that will follow the horrible battle of Armageddon. Birds will clean the earth of the dead bodies—victims of that holocaust.

Just as JEHOVAH TSEBAOTH is the Lord of the feathered hosts, He is also the Lord of the animal hosts:

> *The wolf also shall dwell with the lamb, and the leopard shall lie down with the kid; and the calf and the young lion and the fatling together; and a little child shall lead them* (Isaiah 11:6).

It will be so peaceful during the millennial reign of Christ because He is the Lord of animals, and He will cause the animals to be at peace with one another. The entire ecological system will be transformed because God is Lord of the animals.

When Wally and I first started in the ministry, I taught a soul winning course and would take people door to door. If no one attended my classes, I would go out and knock on doors anyway.

I hated going to some of those places because they had the meanest dogs. It was at this time that I began my ministry of "rebuking dogs"! I would walk into places where big signs boldly announced, **"Beware of Dog."** If a dog approached I would rebuke him in the name of Jesus. Not one dog bit me! Why? Because JEHOVAH TSEBAOTH is the Lord of the hosts of animals and the Lord of the hosts of people. He is *our* Lord of Hosts. We are a peculiar people whom God protects—we're not alone in the battle.

A visiting speaker at our church testified one night how

JEHOVAH TSEBAOTH had protected her during an evangelistic tour to the eastern bloc countries. While she and her husband were in Poland, the Holy Spirit instructed her to go with a portion of the team into East Germany. Her husband was to continue to work in Poland. After several days of ministry in East Germany, she boarded a train to return to her husband.

She was totally unfamiliar with that part of East Germany, and after switching trains several times, was unsure where to go next. When the train stopped, everyone disembarked. Thinking that she probably was to do the same, she stepped off the train and went over to ask directions from two Russian policemen who were in that particular station.

The men immediately ordered her back onto the train, which, by this time, was totally abandoned. They followed her on board and began several hours of intense interrogation and physical abuse. When they did not get the information they wanted, the policemen decided to arrest her and take her to KGB headquarters.

Unaware that the evangelist was fluent in the Russian language, the policemen spoke openly: "Why should we go to the expense of keeping this woman in jail?" the head officer asked the guard. "Let's just put her at the mercy of our German Shepherds."

"Good idea," the guard responded. "Then we will be rid of her!"

These demoniacally controlled men were well aware that their German Shepherds were no ordinary house pets. They were trained killers that, upon command, would instantly gouge out a person's throat.

So the policemen shoved this helpless woman into the cage

where the dogs were kept and shouted, "Kill her!"

Immediately, one dog leaped toward her throat. In that same terror-stricken moment, she pointed at the dog and heard herself shout, **"I resist you in the name of the Lord Jesus Christ!"**

Instantly the dog dropped back and lay transfixed on the floor. The Russian police kept giving the command, **"Kill! Kill! Kill!"** But the Word of God had already proceeded from the woman's mouth. The German Shepherds were immobilized. JEHOVAH TSEBAOTH—the Lord of the animal hosts—had delivered this brave woman from the killer dogs.

But that wasn't the end of this woman's encounter with JEHOVAH TSEBAOTH! Soon, a third uniformed official, whose appearance was totally different from the Russian guards, entered the room. This man had a kind face that radiated God's love and mercy. Quietly he unlocked the cage and motioned the woman to walk toward the door. "Come with me," he said.

The kindly official ushered the woman into a private room where he served her a four-course meal, which was a welcome refreshment since she had eaten nothing in over twenty-four hours. Then the guard escorted her through several check points and through the maze of transfers necessary for her to return to Poland. She could have never found her way without this stranger.

When the official had placed her safely on the last train, he handed her a first-class ticket—the finest seating the train had to offer. Then he looked into her grateful eyes and spoke a final exhortation, "In all that you do, always, always remember: remain faithful to your Lord Jesus Christ to the very end." Then he vanished before her eyes! She had been in the presence of an angel of JEHOVAH TSEBAOTH—Lord of the angelic hosts!

So God had manifested Himself to this woman in three ways: as the Lord of the animal hosts, as the Lord of the angelic hosts, and, because she served as one of His warriors, He had protected her as one in the ranks of the hosts of saints.

As born-again believers, we, too, serve the Lord of hosts of saints. God is our Commander-in-Chief, and although we will always have a battle to fight, remember:

"... *the battle is the LORD'S* , ... " (I Samuel 17:47).

I doubt that even one soldier who fought in World War II ever said, "This is my personal war with Hitler." Our government never said, "This is a war between the Americans and the Nazis." No, everyone knew that World War II was a war between the Allies and the Axis powers. Although it was not their personal war, those soldiers were involved in a very personal way: their very lives were threatened.

Likewise, we are in a battle; and we fight a very real enemy— Satan. Although we are involved personally, we are not in a **personal** battle with Satan. On the contrary, Satan's battle is with the Lord. We simply stand together as God's warriors. He is JEHOVAH TSEBAOTH, Who is pleased to call us— His army—more than conquerors through Jesus Christ!

The Lord of Hosts does not command some bedraggled group of soldiers. JEHOVAH TSEBAOTH's hosts are an awesome display of His power and ability. And He sees each of us as unique individuals with magnificent qualities and attributes—loyal and dedicated to Him, and Him alone!

That's who **you** are! Under JEHOVAH TSEBAOTH'S command, you are a mighty warrior of great authority and ability through Jesus Christ. He has made you **more** than a conqueror!

## JEHOVAH TSEBAOTH

*"Thus the heavens and the earth were finished, and all the **host** of them"* (Genesis 2:1).

*And this man went up out of his city yearly to worship and to sacrifice unto the LORD of **hosts** in Shiloh. And the two sons of Eli, Hophni and Phinehas, the priests of the LORD, were there* (I Samuel 1:3).

*Thou, even thou, art LORD alone; thou hast made heaven, the heaven of heavens, with all their **host**, the earth, and all things that are therein, the seas, and all that is therein, and thou preservest them all; and the host of heaven worshipeth thee* (Nehemiah 9:6).

*"The LORD of **hosts** is with us; the God of Jacob is our refuge. Selah"* (Psalms 46:7).

*"Bless ye the LORD, all ye his **hosts**; ye ministers of his, that do his pleasure"* (Psalms 103:21).

*"And one cried unto another, and said, Holy, holy, holy, is the LORD of **hosts**: the whole earth is full of his glory"* (Isaiah 6:3).

*Lift up your eyes on high, and behold who hath created these things, that bringeth out their **host** by number: he calleth them all by names by the* greatness of his might, for that he is strong in power; not one faileth (Isaiah 40:26).

But, O LORD of **hosts**, that judgest righteously, that triest the reins and the heart, let me see thy vengeance on them: for unto thee have I revealed my cause (Jeremiah 11:20).

Yea, every pot in Jerusalem and in Judah shall be holiness unto the LORD of **hosts**: and all they that sacrifice shall come and take of them, and seethe therein: and in that day there shall be no more the Canaanite in the house of the LORD of **hosts** (Zechariah 14:21).

"And as Esaias said before, Except the Lord of **Sabaoth** had left us a seed, we had been as Sodoma, and been made like unto Gomorrha" (Romans 9:29).

Behold, the hire of the labourers who have reaped down your fields, which is of you kept back by fraud, crieth: and the cries of them which have reaped are entered into the ears of the Lord of **Sabaoth** (James 5:4).

# Chapter Fifteen

# JEHOVAH MAKKEH

Jesus is the cornerstone in the Kingdom of God, and born-again believers are the lively stones that help to form that building. When we were first born again, we were awkwardly shaped because of the toll that sin had taken on our lives. Our minds had not been renewed to the Word; therefore, we still had worldly ideas and attitudes. So the Lord began to mold us and shape us according to His Word so that we would fit perfectly into our place within the Body.

This is JEHOVAH MAKKEH, "the Lord, our Smiter," and His purpose is to shape and perfect us into smooth, lively stones that are molded together and operate in a unified manner.

Psalms 51:17 says, "*. . . a broken and a contrite heart, O God, thou wilt not despise.*" If we are not willing to be "broken," to surrender our wills to Him, so that He can mold us into place, then we will be crushed. By whom? The devil and our circumstances.

The devil wants to crush you—to shatter your life—but God wants to mold you so that you can lead a successful, productive life. Yes, God does smite us—He molds, chisels, and smooths us; but He NEVER crushes us.

You may ask, "Marilyn, why am I able to take correction at some times, but I rebel against it at other times?" We will all be corrected from time to time, but it's our attitude toward the correction that makes the difference. In this chapter I am going to show you how always to benefit when JEHOVAH MAKKEH chastens you.

When I was in the ninth grade, the teacher I had for Latin "smote me hard!" One day in particular I was called to the blackboard to do conjunctions. I didn't know them well, and the teacher said to me, "You dummy! Why don't you ever study!"

I was so sensitive at that age and to receive such harsh criticism absolutely humiliated me. You may be thinking, "Well, he shouldn't have been so cruel." But wait, a lot of things happen to us that shouldn't, so we must choose—do we fall apart and give up, or do we shape up and learn from the experience?

My first reaction was to cry—which embarrassed me even more. I never wanted to face that teacher or anyone in that school ever again. After a few minutes the teacher said that he wanted to see me after school. I spent the rest of the day worrying about what he was going to say to me. By that afternoon when the last school bell had rung, I once again dissolved into tears.

The teacher said, "Now, Marilyn, stop crying. I'm hard on you because I see that you have some ability in foreign languages. I'm going to continue to be hard on you so that you will live up to your potential and possibly accomplish something in this field someday."

That teacher did more for me than any other public school teacher I ever had. I later went to college and received a degree to teach foreign languages. Instead of allowing those circumstances to smash me, I learned from the experience and God used it to shape my life. Today in the ministry I continue to use teaching techniques that I learned in college.

Let's look at some biblical accounts of men who were chastened by the Lord. Second Chronicles 25 relates the story of a man who was corrected and paid the price of his correction. The first time he allowed the Lord to correct him, the man was wonderfully blessed; yet the second time, the man did not receive the Lord's correction and was crushed by his circumstances!

Amaziah was the king of Judah. The reign of his father Joash was marked by both success and disaster! The early period of Joash's life was heavily influenced by the noble priest Jehoiada. Upon his coronation the king and his people covenanted to worship God alone. Immediately, Baal's temple in Jerusalem was destroyed and Mosaic Law was reinstated. Joash repaired the Temple, and as long as Jehoiada lived, the law was observed carefully.

However, Joash's moral and spiritual decline began at Jehoiada's death. Almost immediately, Joash's lack of commitment to God began to show. Some of the princes of Judah persuaded Joash to readmit Baalism into the kingdom.

Instead of leaning on Jehovah and receiving His strength, Joash depended on other human beings for strength and guidance—which marked the collapse of his reign. Jehoiada's son Zechariah, with whom Joash had been raised, tried to correct Joash with the word, "Don't hurt our nation by turning to idolatry."

Now at this point, Joash could have said, "I have been wrong. I must repent and listen to godly counsel." Unfortunately, however, Joash became prideful and rebellious. He instigated Zechariah's execution for protesting the new swing into idolatry.

But judgment quickly followed: before the end of the year, a small Syrian army invaded Judah and killed the princes who had spearheaded the movement into idolatry. Joash's superior army was defeated because both he and his advisors had forsaken God. After the defeat, Joash was murdered by his own servants.

Training and chastening come from God's hand. When the devil tries to crush us with circumstances, we can fall upon the Rock, Jesus Christ, and find a way to surmount the very difficulties that are trying to overwhelm us.

After Joash's death, his son Amaziah assumed the throne. During this time the tiny country of Edom declared war on Judah. Amaziah gathered a large army consisting of 300,000 men who loved God just as Amaziah did. However, someone came to Amaziah and declared, "I've heard that the Edomites have hired mercenaries to fight with them, and now they have a huge army. You had better hire some soldiers too. Otherwise we will be defeated."

Worldly people will often offer counsel, but the Bible says:

> *"Blessed is the man that walketh not in the counsel*
> *of the ungodly, . . . "* (Psalms 1:1).

If Amaziah had only had himself and one other man to fight, it would have been sufficient. Why? Because Judah had God's favor and blessing.

But Amaziah became fearful and heeded the ungodly advice: he went to Israel—the ten tribes to the north that worshiped Baal and golden calves—and, at great expense, hired 100,000 mercenaries to join his army. Just as oil and water do not mix, neither do the ungodly and the godly:

> *"Can two walk together, except they be agreed?"*
> (Amos 3:3).

As the army was moving to the battle field, a prophet warned Amaziah:

> *. . . O king, let not the army of Israel go with thee;*
> *for the LORD is not with Israel, to wit, with all the*

*children of Ephraim. But if thou wilt go, do it, be strong for the battle: God shall make thee fall before the enemy: for God hath power to help, and to cast down* (II Chronicles 25:7,8).

Amaziah had paid a great sum of money to hire the mercenaries; but reluctantly, he agreed to dismiss them. Sometimes it costs us to be true to God; but if we will pay the price, we will be abundantly blessed.

Once, when I was in school, I cheated on a homework assignment. God dealt with me severely; yet I was afraid to tell my teacher, because I knew that I would receive a failing grade. Finally, I made the decision to tell my teacher the truth. I did receive a failing grade for that particular assignment; yet at the end of the semester, my overall grade for the class was an "A." God had allowed the many good grades I received to overcome the one failure.

If you do the right thing, God will fight for you. If you will fall on the Rock, Jesus Christ, you will always be successful. However, if you let rocky circumstances fall on you, then you will be crushed!

Amaziah was willing to fall on the Rock: he sent back the 100,000 mercenaries. Then Amaziah and his 300,000 godly soldiers won the battle against the Edomites and took great spoil. Unlike his prideful father, Amaziah received the prophet's correction, threw himself on God's mercy and power, and overcame his circumstances to experience an astounding victory!

Unfortunately, the sweet savor of victory was short-lived. Instead of destroying the Edomites' pagan idols, Amaziah foolishly accepted them as part of his plunder:

> *Now it came to pass, after that Amaziah was come*
> *from the slaughter of the Edomites, that he brought*
> *the gods of the children of Seir, and set them up*
> *to be his gods, and bowed down himself before them,*
> *and burned incense unto them* (II Chronicles 25:14).

Again the Lord sent a prophet to Amaziah to counsel him and try to guide him back to righteousness. But this time Amaziah did not receive the prophet's correction. So the prophet announced:

> *". . . I know that God hath determined to destroy*
> *thee, because thou hast done this, and hast not*
> *hearkened unto my counsel"* (II Chronicles 25:16).

But Amaziah's ego knew no limits. After his victory over the Edomites, Amaziah had fallen into pride and had begun to think he could overpower any army—with or without God's blessing! However, the Word says that pride precedes a fall, and Amaziah was no exception. Later his small army was soundly beaten by Israel's superior army: it destroyed a portion of Jerusalem's wall, plundered the Temple, and took numerous hostages. Amaziah himself fled for his life to Lachish, where he lived until his enemies assassinated him.

Amaziah failed because he had hardened his heart toward God and refused to receive His correction. But we can learn from Amaziah's mistake. If we will accept the Lord's chastening and allow Him to mold and shape us, we will fit well into the Body of Christ. However, if we refuse the Lord's chastening, we will suffer staggering defeats.

Now you may say, "Marilyn, I don't believe that God destroys people." You're right; He doesn't. But when we choose disobedience over obedience, essentially, we are choosing death over life and bringing a curse upon our own lives.

Often after encountering misfortune, people will say, "Look what God did to me." However, they should say, "Look what I've done to myself." God cannot bless sin. Whenever people sin they bring a curse upon themselves.

The prophet Ezekiel was the first person to call the Lord JEHOVAH MAKKEH:

> *And mine eye shall not spare, neither will I have pity: I will recompense thee according to thy ways and thine abominations that are in the midst of thee; and ye shall know that I am the LORD that smiteth* (Ezekiel 7:9).

Ezekiel 9 presents a situation in which the Lord smote Judah:

> *And to the others he said in mine hearing, Go ye after him through the city, and smite: let not your eye spare, neither have ye pity: Slay utterly old and young, both maids, and little children, and women: but come not near any man upon whom is the mark; and begin at my sanctuary. Then they began at the ancient men which were before the house* (Ezekiel 9:5,6).

Judah had turned away from God to worship idols. In a vision, Ezekiel saw the Lord tell an angel to smite all the people who had turned to idolatry; but the angel was to spare anyone who had the Lord's mark. These were godly people who were willing to pray and intercede for the idolatrous people in that day.

Judah was smitten because it had turned to idolatry. When Babylon seized Judah, those people who weren't killed by the knife or by fire had to flee for their very lives. But the people who were marked by God—those who had contrite spirits and had surrendered to God rather than to idols—were protected during the siege. God will defend and protect anyone who will keep his or her heart open to Him.

Proverbs 19:25 says, *"Smite a scorner, and the simple will beware: . . . . "* Has anyone ever scorned you? Do you know people who continually scorn Christianity, "Oh, I would never be a Christian! They don't drink; they don't smoke; they're all a bunch of weirdos!" The apostle Paul was a scorner. Oh, he absolutely hated Christians, and he continually bragged about the terrible things he did to them. But, one day, while traveling on the road to Damascus, Paul was "smitten" by God.

Why did God smite Paul? Because that was the only way that God could get Paul's attention.

Paul asked, "Who are you, Lord?"

And the Lord said, "I am Jesus Christ. Why do you continue to persecute Christians? When you persecute them, you persecute Me."

Paul learned his lesson; he never scorned after that experience. And he became one of the greatest men ever to walk on this earth.

Now God may never slap you to the ground to make you listen to Him, but He will chasten you. How will God do this? Will He chasten you through sickness, disease, or poverty? No! He will correct you with His Word. Don't ever think, "I'm sick. God must be chastening me." That's not God! The devil uses illness and poverty to crush you; God trains only with His Word.

People may also smite you:

> *"Let the righteous smite me; it shall be a kindness: and let him reprove me; it shall be an excellent oil, which shall not break my head: ... "* (Psalms 141:5).

Godly correction will not hurt you! It will be as a soothing oil that may produce a miracle in your life. Sometimes it may sting your flesh a little to be corrected, but your spirit will rejoice, and you will be a better person for it.

People are not always going to say what you want to hear. But if you surrender your flesh to the Lord and accept godly counsel, you will see the miraculous.

You may ask, "Marilyn, how do I handle correction and receive a miracle?" Through Jesus Christ:

> *Surely he hath borne our griefs, and carried our sorrows: yet we did esteem him stricken, smitten of God, and afflicted. But he was wounded for our transgressions, he was bruised for our iniquities: the chastisement of our peace was upon him; and with his stripes we are healed* (Isaiah 53:4,5).

God smote Jesus with our sins, our griefs, sorrows, and sicknesses. Why? So that we wouldn't have to be smitten with them. It pleased God to smite Jesus rather than us:

> *Yet it pleased the LORD to bruise him; he hath put him to grief: when thou shalt make his soul an offering for sin, he shall see his seed, he shall prolong his days, and the pleasure of the LORD shall prosper*

*in his hand* (Isaiah 53:10).

Jesus has come between anything that would try to crush you:

*Awake, O sword, against my shepherd, and against the man that is my fellow, saith the LORD of hosts: smite the shepherd, and the sheep shall be scattered: and I will turn mine hand upon the little ones* (Zechariah 13:7).

*" . . . 'All ye shall be offended because of me this night: for it is written, I will smite the shepherd, and the sheep . . . ' "* (Matthew 26:31).

Who is the Shepherd? Jesus Christ. He stood in our place and accepted the penalty for our sins. When we allow circumstances to upset us, we have missed the smitten One Who came to stand between us and our heartbreak.

Jesus didn't say, "I have come to break your heart." No, He said, "I have come to heal the brokenhearted."

I am reminded of a situation several years ago that involved a woman who offended me so much that even the thought of facing her upset me. One day after my husband Wally had preached an excellent service, this woman said to me, "I never listen to Wally's sermons when he wears that gold ring on his little finger."

"Why not?" I asked somewhat perplexed.

"Because that ring has an idol on it. Who gave it to him anyway?"

"I gave it to him," I said, "and it doesn't have an idol on it."

Another time the same woman said to me, "That dress looks

terrible on you! I'd like to have a pastor's wife that looks like something other than a slop bucket!"

Finally this woman moved to another state, and I felt so relieved! But a few years later I spoke at a convention in the city to which the woman had moved. When she heard about the convention, the woman wrote me a letter stating that she could hardly wait to see me!

Immediately, I thought, "Well, I can surely wait to see you!" Then I prayed, "Lord, this woman only wants to see me so she can criticize me. How can I go to that city without seeing her?"

But the Lord began to deal with my heart, "If you'll let Me stand between yourself and her criticisms, I will bring you through this and restore your relationship with this woman."

At the convention, I decided to relax and let the Lord deal with my problem. Regardless of what she said, I decided to let Jesus deal with it. When I saw the woman, all my previous apprehensions fell away. We embraced warmly and cried tears of joy. Why? Because I had allowed Jesus to enter into the situation, and He made it sweet.

Do you allow Jesus to enter into your difficult situations? Or do you carry the burden on your own shoulders? If you try to carry your burdens, you will be crushed under the weight of them.

In Exodus 15:22-27 the Israelites had begun to grumble and complain because of the lack of food and water on their journey to the Promised Land. During one three-day journey southward into the wilderness of Shur, they found no water until they reached Marah. There the Israelites discovered that the water was bitter and unfit for consumption.

However, the waters of Marah were sweetened when Moses,

at God's direction, cast a tree into them. Like Moses, when we enter bitter situations, we need to turn to God for direction. Jesus accepted all our bitter situations on a tree—the Cross! He was smitten for us, and if we will allow JEHOVAH MAKKEH to enter our situations, He will make them sweet.

How does JEHOVAH MAKKEH work in our lives? He corrects us with His Word and inspires other godly people to correct us as well. His gentle molding and chiseling shapes us into the image of His dear Son Jesus Christ and helps us to fit perfectly in our positions within the Body of Christ.

JEHOVAH MAKKEH, the Lord, our Smiter, also took our "correction" on the Cross: God smote Jesus with our sins, griefs, and sorrows so that we wouldn't have to be smitten with them. Now we can cast our burdens on Him when others' unfair criticisms hurt or offend us. Allow JEHOVAH MAKKEH to do His perfect work in you today.

## JEHOVAH MAKKEH

*"Surely he hath borne our griefs, and carried our sorrows: yet we did esteem him stricken, **smitten** of God, and afflicted"* (Isaiah 53:4).

*"He giveth his cheek to him that **smiteth** him: he is filled full with reproach"* (Lamentations 3:30).

*And mine eye shall not spare, neither will I have pity: I will recompense thee according to thy ways and thine abominations that are in the midst of thee; and ye shall know that I am the LORD that **smiteth*** (Ezekiel 7:9).

*Behold, therefore I have **smitten** mine hand at thy dishonest gain which thou hast made, and at thy blood which hath been in the midst of thee* (Ezekiel 22:13).

*Awake, O sword, against my shepherd, and against the man that is my fellow, saith the LORD of host: **smite** the shepherd, and the sheep shall be scattered: and I will turn mine hand upon the little ones* (Zechariah 13:7).

*And he shall turn the heart of the fathers to the children, and the heart of the children to their fathers, lest I come and **smite** the earth with a curse* (Malachi 4:6).

# Chapter Sixteen

# JEHOVAH GMOLAH

**D**aily we are faced with choices. Some of the decisions we make seem ordinary and inconsequential—what to wear, whether to have a sandwich or soup for lunch, whether to take the freeway or drive side streets home from work. Yet other decisions we make are absolutely crucial and can have long-term affects on our lives: which occupation to choose, whom to marry, or where to make our homes. And even more importantly, we make crucial spiritual decisions to obey God's Word and choose His blessing or disobey His Word and accept the consequences.

In this chapter we are going to study JEHOVAH GMOLAH, the Lord of Recompenses. To recompense means "to repay, to reward, or to compensate." The Lord always compensates the choices we make. The first biblical reference to JEHOVAH GMOLAH is found in Jeremiah 51:56 when God promises that Babylon will reap whatever it sows during its siege on Jerusalem:

> *Because the spoiler is come upon her, even upon Babylon, and her mighty men are taken, every one of their bows is broken: for the LORD God of recompences shall surely requite.*

And God did compensate Babylon for this attack. Approximately 70 years later, Babylon was sieged by the Medes and the Persians.

Moses also encountered JEHOVAH GMOLAH, although Moses didn't call God by this name. Moses had been adopted by Hatshepsut, the daughter of Pharaoh. History records that Hatshepsut was a brilliant woman, but Egyptian custom maintained that no woman could reign. Hatshepsut's half-brother, who was practically mentally handicapped, would be the next Pharaoh—simply because he was male. To ensure strong leadership during the next generation, Pharaoh arranged a marriage between Hatshepsut and her half-brother.

Hatshepsut absolutely hated being married to her half-brother, so she poisoned him. Since they had no sons to assume leadership, Hatshepsut herself ruled Egypt.

But one day, as she was bathing in the Nile, she noticed a tiny ark floating past her, and she sent one of her maids to retrieve it:

> *And when she had opened it, she saw the child: and, behold, the babe wept. And she had compassion on him, and said, This is one of the Hebrews' children* (Exodus 2:6).

Hatshepsut named the child Moses and began grooming him to become the next Egyptian Pharaoh. But God had not chosen Moses to be an Egyptian Pharaoh; rather, God had chosen Moses to deliver the Israelites from Egyptian bondage.

Moses was faced with a choice. Would he decide to follow Hatshepsut and become the next Pharaoh of Egypt—the most advanced civilization in the world at that time? Or would he choose to follow God and deliver the Israelites from bondage? Moses weighed his choices carefully. He needed to decide which alternative would offer the greatest reward.

Moses had some weighty choices to make—just as we do today. But Moses knew that, regardless of his decision, he would receive the recompense of that choice. Hebrews 11:26 reveals Moses' decision:

> *"Esteeming the reproach of Christ greater riches*

> *than the treasures in Egypt: for he had respect*
> *unto the recompence of the reward."*

Moses said, "I believe I'll get more by following God." Do you believe he made the right choice? I do! If Moses had chosen to become the next Pharaoh, only a few historians who studied Egyptian history would have remembered his name. But Moses' compensation for choosing to follow God included writing the Pentateuch and appearing on the Mount of Transfiguration with Jesus Christ!

Following Jesus always offers the richest rewards, because people who follow Him change the course of history. How? By bringing light into darkness. Who knows? By teaching a children's Sunday school class, you may be helping to mold and train a future president of the United States.

If we put our confidence in JEHOVAH GMOLAH, we will reap tremendous compensation because He is the Lord of Recompenses! Hebrews 10:35 says, *"Cast not away therefore your confidence, which hath great recompence of reward."*

I have seen JEHOVAH GMOLAH at work in my own life. Each weekday morning my husband Wally and I go to our church for early morning prayer. One morning I was particularly concerned about one of our loved ones, and I said, "Lord, I have prayed and prayed and prayed. Sometimes I get tired of praying yet never seeing an answer."

And the Lord reminded me of Hebrews 11:6:

> *But without faith it is impossible to please him: for*
> *he that cometh to God must believe that he is, and*
> *that he is a rewarder of them that diligently*
> *seek him.*

God said, "Marilyn, you have to believe that I am and that I reward those who seek Me. Do you believe that I am?"

I answered, "Oh, yes! I do, Lord!"

"Do you seek Me diligently?" He continued.

Again I answered, "Yes, Father! I pray every day!"

"So what do you get?"

"The reward!"

Be diligent in your prayer life. Set aside an hour each day to pray, and faithfully keep it. If you maintain great confidence in JEHOVAH GMOLAH, you will receive a great reward.

What else is necessary to receive great rewards from JEHOVAH GMOLAH? Giving! Romans 11:35 says, *"Or who hath first given to him, and it shall be recompensed unto him again?"* If you give to God, your giving will be recompensed to you.

For many years church leaders taught that it was scriptural to give, but they never mentioned that people would receive anything in return for their giving. Leaders often said, "Through the tithe, you are paying God what you owe Him." It's true—we do owe God the tithe. However, few of the leaders ever said, "If you tithe, God will open the windows of heaven to bless you." Who is the best paymaster? JEHOVAH GMOLAH, the Lord of Recompenses!

We should always expect to receive when we give. No employee would work for a company, give 40 hours or more a week, without expecting to receive a paycheck. Likewise, we should not give our tithes to God without expecting compensation. If you sow into God's kingdom, JEHOVAH GMOLAH will compensate your giving.

I often hear people say, "I work my fingers to the bone, but I never get anything. Someone else always gets the raises and promotions." But God has promised that what our hands do shall prosper:

> *"A man shall be satisfied with good by the fruit of his mouth: and the recompence of a man's hands shall be rendered unto him"* (Proverbs 12:14).

Always expect to be repaid when you work—whether it's at home, in an office, or at school. JEHOVAH GMOLAH ensures that you will be compensated for your labor.

Holy living always brings rewards from JEHOVAH GMOLAH:

> *"Behold, the righteous shall be recompensed in the earth: much more the wicked and the sinner"* (Proverbs 11:31).

A young woman in our congregation was in the ninth grade when she made a decision not to drink alcohol. Over 75 percent of the students in her school drank heavily, so she was often quite tempted to join them in order to feel accepted. But she remained firm in her decision not to drink.

During the next two and one half years, she was labeled a "goody two shoes" and was left out of almost every social event at her school. But during her senior year, many of the students said, "We wish we had made the same decision not to drink. We see now that you were right and we were wrong."

God began to bless that young woman in every area of her life. She went away to college and was a straight "A" student. God is using her as a missionary. One summer she appealed for money for the missions' field and received double the amount that she needed! Remember, it pays to be righteous.

JEHOVAH GMOLAH will also recompense us for the good things that we sow in our children:

> *Thou shewest lovingkindness unto thousands, and recompensest the iniquity of the fathers into the bosom of their children after them: the Great, the Mighty God, the LORD of hosts, is his name* (Jeremiah 32:18).

But the harvest doesn't stop with our children. We will also reap through our grandchildren for one thousand generations. That means that one thousand generations from now, if Jesus tarries, you will have descendants who are serving God with all their hearts.

Each year Wally plants tomatoes, and we only expect to harvest tomatoes during the summer months. In the fall the vines will wither and die. But when we sow into the spiritual realm, God's kingdom, we reap continual harvests. It never freezes in His garden, and the plants never wither and die. The seed will continue to reproduce and bring continuous harvests.

Sow well into your children—enroll them in Christian schools, speak the Word to them, pray with them, take them to church—because you will receive an abundant reward.

This spiritual truth can also work in reverse:

> *". . . ye fathers, provoke not your children to wrath: but bring them up in the nurture and admonition of the Lord"* (Ephesians 6:4).

Do you know why most adults have problems with depression?

Because their fathers provoked these people to wrath when they were younger. Of course, children must be trained and disciplined—but only with nurture and love.

We must remember that JEHOVAH GMOLAH also compensates transgressions and disobedience:

> *For if the word spoken by angels was stedfast, and every transgression and disobedience received a just recompence of reward; How shall we escape, if we neglect so great salvation; . . .* (Hebrews 2:2,3).

If we refuse the Word and sow evil, we will reap that too:

> *". . . when lust hath conceived, it bringeth forth sin: and sin, when it is finished, bringeth forth death"* (James 1:15).

Let's compare this scripture to conceiving a child. Everyone wants a healthy baby, and it is devastating to everyone involved when a baby is stillborn. When we sow sin in our lives, it is the same as conceiving a dead baby. The day will come when we will give birth to that sin and reap the awful compensation for it.

Another transgression that JEHOVAH GMOLAH recompenses is vanity:

> *"Let not him that is deceived trust in vanity: for vanity shall be his recompence"* (Job 15:31).

Our society today places far too much emphasis on appearance. I believe that everyone should look his or her best, but when appearance becomes the central focus of our lives, we are sowing into vanity. And by doing this, we become nicely painted, albeit empty, shells.

Many people live for recreation, which is another form of vanity. They think, "I live for the weekends so I can ski" or "Summer is the only season I like because I can sail on the lake." These people sow only into entertainment, and unfortunately they reap a meager reward.

Now, I'm not saying that it is wrong to relax or to look good; however, I am saying that we should not focus primarily on entertainment or appearances. How much of your time is spent pursuing frivolity and vanity? How much of your time is wisely directed toward creativity and productivity? If you sow into godly things that will help to mature you, then you will see good results.

Vengeance also has its recompense. If we begin to seek vengeance—even subtly—we will reap the consequences of it:

> *To me belongeth vengeance, and recompence; their foot shall slide in due time: for the day of their calamity is at hand, and the things that shall come upon them make haste. If I whet my glittering sword, and mine hand take hold on judgment; I will render vengeance to mine enemies, and will reward them that hate me. Rejoice, O ye nations, with his people: for he will avenge the blood of his servants, and will render vengeance to his adversaries, and will be merciful unto his land, and to his people* (Deuteronomy 32:35,41,43).

Both vengeance and recompense belong to the Lord. God

has promised to heal our hurts and to enable us to overcome crippling emotional blows from others. What happens when we try to avenge ourselves? We put ourselves in God's place; we try to be JEHOVAH GMOLAH. Then God says, "You've taken control, so I can't intervene in the situation."

We must choose between revenge and reconciliation. Revenge may seem sweet to the flesh, but in reality, it is costly. Allow God to take vengeance and bring reconciliation into your situations.

It grieves me to see what the communists are doing in countries like Ethiopia and Poland. But JEHOVAH GMOLAH will compensate communism. We can worry ourselves into a frenzy over world events, but worrying will do no good. Only JEHOVAH GMOLAH, the Lord of Recompenses, can avenge evil and bring reconciliation.

What motivates us to seek revenge? Wrath:

> *"Dearly beloved, avenge not yourselves, but rather give place unto wrath: for it is written, Vengeance is mine; I will repay, saith the Lord"* (Romans 12:19).

If we don't allow ourselves to be provoked to wrath, we will not take the next step: revenge.

Absolutely, God will bless your situations and bring reconciliation to broken relationships—if you will allow Him to intervene. I have faced three major conflicts with others in my life. Unquestionably, I was at fault as well as the people with whom I had the conflicts. I thought, "God, these people are so wrong. And I want to help You set them straight." But my involvement only magnified the problem. However, when I withdrew and repented for interfering and believing that they were more at fault than me, JEHOVAH GMOLAH was able to intervene. Each conflict was beautifully resolved, and today these people are among my closest friends.

In the Old Testament Ruth, a Moabitess, could have allowed conflict and bitterness to overwhelm her. Instead she chose to follow God, and JEHOVAH GMOLAH, the Lord of Recompenses, sustained and blessed her:

> *"The LORD recompense thy work, and a full reward be given thee of the LORD God of Israel, under whose wings thou art come to trust"* (Ruth 2:12).

Ruth's husband and father-in-law had both died, and her mother-in-law Naomi had decided to return to Bethlehem. What was Ruth going to do all alone in Moab? Ruth could have been bitter—at her mother-in-law, at circumstances, even at the Lord—but Ruth chose not to be offended.

Ruth weighed her alternatives and decided that it was more profitable to trust the Lord. She chose to go with Naomi and to trust in Naomi's God rather than in the Moabite idols.

Immediately, however, the two women suffered a food shortage. It was springtime in Bethlehem, and the barley harvest was just beginning. Ruth sought work in the fields of a wealthy Ephrathite named Boaz, who was a relative of her late husband:

> *And Ruth the Moabitess said unto Naomi, Let me now go to the field, and glean ears of corn after him in whose sight I shall find grace. And she said unto her, Go, my daughter* (Ruth 2:2).

So Ruth went to glean in the fields. And the owner Boaz noticed her and fell in love. Eventually, Ruth married Boaz and had a baby of her own. Obed, the son of Ruth and Boaz, became the grandfather of David, the ancestor of Jesus Christ.

JEHOVAH GMOLAH wonderfully recompensed Ruth for her commitment to Him. But remember, whenever you commit to the Lord, a testing time will follow. At first it appeared that Ruth and Naomi would starve in Bethlehem or, at the very best, become common street beggars. But Ruth continued to trust in the Lord, and at exactly the right time, she received her reward. Instead of becoming a beggar, she became one of the wealthiest women in Bethlehem and ended up in the lineage of Jesus Christ.

Several years ago a particular 30-year-old woman came to me for advice and prayer. "Oh, Marilyn," she cried, "I'm afraid I'll never marry! I don't want to be alone!" So I prayed with her and she seemed better.

When she turned 31, the same thing happened. "I'm 31 now," she cried, "and I don't have anybody." At 32, she became so depressed that she even stopped attending church. We called several times to encourage her, but she remained despondent.

I absolutely dreaded her thirty-third birthday! As in previous years, she came to see me, but this time she wasn't crying. Instead, she said, "I'm going to serve Jesus with all my heart. If He brings me a husband, fine; but if He doesn't bring me a husband, that's fine too." The woman's entire attitude changed. She was willing to do anything in her commitment to serve the Lord wholeheartedly: she typed my teaching notes, worked with our Sunday school curriculum, and even baby-sat my children.

One Sunday afternoon, a young man from another church

was a guest at our church picnic. As we were visiting, he asked, "Who is that pretty lady over there?" It was the young woman who had dedicated her life completely to God.

Not wanting to miss an opportunity to do some matchmaking, I responded, "Let me introduce you."

Not long afterward, they were married, and today they have a beautiful family.

Likewise, you need to commit to the Lord wholeheartedly. He will bring you a husband, a wife, financial security, or whatever is lacking in your life. He is JEHOVAH GMOLAH, the Lord of Recompenses, and He will reward your devotion.

JEHOVAH GMOLAH wants to bless our families abundantly, and, to achieve that purpose, God has given us specific guidelines on ordering our family relationships:

> *Wives, submit yourselves unto your own husbands, as it is fit in the Lord. Husbands, love your wives, and be not bitter against them. Children, obey your parents in all things: for this is well pleasing unto the Lord. Fathers, provoke not your children to anger, lest they be discouraged. Servants, obey in all things your masters according to the flesh; not with eyeservice, as men-pleasers; but in singleness of heart, fearing God: And whatsoever ye do, do it heartily, as to the Lord, and not unto men; Knowing that of the Lord ye shall receive the reward of the inheritance: for ye serve the Lord Christ* (Colossians 3:18-24).

Sometimes we may get angry with our spouses, our parents, our employers; but it is important we obey them and love them anyway. We should do everything as unto the Lord, because He is the One Who will compensate us. If you obey God's Word, you will receive a great reward. Put your confidence in Him! JEHOVAH GMOLAH—the Lord of Recompenses, guarantees a wonderful harvest of blessings!

Do you expect compensation for the choices that you make? Daily, as you choose God's Word, give into the kingdom, or choose righteousness and holiness over your own desires, you can expect JEHOVAH GMOLAH to reward you. Invite Him to bring His abundance into your life by making godly choices. After you taste the fruit of JEHOVAH GMOLAH'S blessing, you will never desire to disobey God's Word again!

## JEHOVAH GMOLAH

*To me belongeth vengeance, and **recompence**; their foot shall slide in due time: for the day of their calamity is at hand, and the things that shall come upon them make haste* (Deuteronomy 32:35).

*"Say not thou, I will **recompense** evil; but wait on the LORD, and he shall save thee"* (Proverbs 20:22).

*Thou shewest lovingkindness unto thousands, and **recompensest** the iniquity of the fathers into the bosom of their children after them: the Great, the Mighty God, the LORD of hosts, is his name* (Jeremiah 32:18).

*Because the spoiler is come upon her, even upon Babylon, and her mighty men are taken, every one of their bows is broken: for the LORD God of **recompences** shall surely requite* (Jeremiah 51:56).

***Recompense** to no man evil for evil. Provide things honest in the sight of all men. If it be possible, as much as lieth in you, live peaceably with all men. Dearly beloved, avenge not yourselves, but rather give place unto wrath: for it is written, Vengeance is mine; I will repay, saith the Lord* (Romans 12:17-19).

*For we know him that hath said, Vengeance belongeth unto me, I will **recompense**, saith the Lord. And again, The Lord shall judge his people* (Hebrews 10:30).

# Chapter Seventeen

# JEHOVAH ELOHAY

# EL-ELOHE-ISRAEL

# JEHOVAH ELOHEENU

In this chapter we are going to study three closely related names of God that reveal Him to us as a very personal God. This personal God is One on Whom we can call when we need a miracle and know that He will work in our behalf to bring us to victory and success. The first name is JEHOVAH ELOHAY, meaning "the Lord, **my** God"; the second, EL-ELOHE-ISRAEL, meaning "the personal God of Israel"; and the third is JEHOVAH ELOHEENU, meaning "the Lord, **our** God."

We often receive some of the best revelations from God when we call out to Him in the midst of a fiery trial. People may say, "My life was in utter turmoil before I received Jesus as my Savior," or "I was in terrible financial straits. In my desperation I called out to God, and He gave me a miracle."

Many people—especially long-time Christians—think it's strange when they experience trials. They often think, "I don't deserve this." But we are not to think it strange when we encounter fiery trials:

> *"Beloved, think it not strange concerning the fiery trial which is to try you, as though some strange thing happened unto you"* (I Peter 4:12).

I don't like it when I experience trials. Nobody does. Yet we are still going to experience them. But in the fire of trial, the genuineness of our faith will be tested and proven to be of infinite worth because it is our faith in God that brings victory:

> *That the trial of your faith, being much more precious than of gold that perisheth, though it be tried with fire, might be found unto praise and*

*honour and glory at the appearing of Jesus Christ*
(I Peter 1:7).

Yes, both worldly people and Christians experience trials, but Christians do not have to be consumed by the fire or even singed by it. They can call upon JEHOVAH ELOHAY, EL-ELOHE-ISRAEL, or JEHOVAH ELOHEENU to rescue them from their circumstances.

God promises that we will not be scorched by the fire; in fact, He promises that we will benefit from it. Now you may ask, "Marilyn, how can we ever benefit from something that is trying to hurt us?" We will benefit, because God promises to reveal Himself to us through our trials:

> *When thou passest through the waters, I will be with thee; and through the rivers, they shall not overflow thee; when thou walkest through the fire, thou shalt not be burned; neither shall the flame kindle upon thee* (Isaiah 43:2).

God is able to deliver us **from** every trial, and He is also able to deliver us **through** every trial. You may have to endure the trial before you receive your miracle, but as the Hebrew children in Daniel 3 discovered, it is well worth the wait.

Shadrach, Meshach, and Abed-nego were cast into a fiery furnace when they refused to worship King Nebuchadnezzar's 90-foot idol. The king was so angry at their "disrespect" that he commanded his servants to make the fire seven times hotter than usual. Nebuchadnezzar was determined to show the three Hebrew children—and anyone else who dared to disobey him—who was boss. But Nebuchadnezzar experienced a phenomenon that absolutely changed his life:

> *Then Nebuchadnezzar the king was astonied, and rose up in haste, and spake, and said unto his counsellors, Did we not cast three men bound into the midst of the fire? . . . Lo, I see four men loose, walking in the midst of the fire, and they have no hurt; and the form of the fourth is like the Son of God* (Daniel 3:24,25).

God Himself entered the fire with the Hebrew children, who would not have experienced this manifestation of God had they not been cast into the furnace. But this miracle affected Nebuchadnezzar and the other witnesses as well:

> *. . . Then Shadrach, Meshach, and Abed-nego, came forth of the midst of the fire. And the princes, governors, and captains, and the king's counsellors, being gathered together, saw these men, upon whose bodies the fire had no power, nor was an hair of their head singed, neither were their coats changed, nor the smell of fire had passed on them* (Daniel 3:26,27).

The king and his princes, governors, captains, and counselors were not believers; yet they witnessed a tremendous miracle and were affected by it. Nebuchadnezzar decreed that no one would speak anything against the true and living God, "*. . . because there is no other God that can deliver after this sort*" (Daniel 3:29).

Quite honestly, the world can often see more of Jesus when

we're experiencing trials than when we're not experiencing them. Who knows who will witness your trial and be affected by it? Perhaps your mayor, governor, or a senator will witness the trial and have their lives transformed. Worldly people need to see Jesus walking with us through the flames of our fiery circumstances. And when they witness the miracles He performs on our behalf, they may think, "Oh, there's hope for me too."

Of course, you could allow the fire of circumstances to over-whelm you. You could awaken in the night and worry yourself into a frenzy, you could bite your nails all the way up to your elbows, or you could even bang your head against the wall. But worry will not keep the fire from scorching you. How do you quench the fire? Hebrews 11:34 says, that **by faith** the heroes of faith *"Quenched the violence of fire, . . . . "* If you will remain steadfast in your faith in JEHOVAH ELOHAY, you will quench the violence of the fire that is trying to overwhelm you.

Several years ago, my mother discovered a lump in one of her breasts; and, to our dismay, the doctor's diagnosis was a malignant tumor. I didn't know much about divine healing at the time, and I chuckled when Mother said she believed that God would heal her. But she wisely ignored my disbelief and remained steadfast in her faith.

One night on a Christian television program, the evangelist asked people who were ill to lay their hands on their television sets while he prayed for their healing. I could barely conceal my astonishment when my mother got up and laid her hands on the TV. But the next day, the growth had disappeared. Later medical x-rays confirmed her belief. My mother quenched the violence of that fire with her faith and received a miracle.

271

My mother's faith in JEHOVAH ELOHAY, "the Lord, **my** God," produced a miracle out of her fiery trial. Likewise, Gideon, through his experience with the Midianites, learned to call upon JEHOVAH ELOHAY.

Gideon was called by God to deliver Israel from its oppressors the Midianites. As Gideon was threshing wheat at his father's house in Ophrah, the angel of the Lord commanded him to destroy Baal's altar. And cowardly Gideon responded, " . . . *'Oh my Lord, wherewith shall I save Israel? behold, my family is poor in Manasseh, and I am the least in my father's house'"* (Judges 6:15). Gideon may have been a coward, but he wasn't a dumb coward! He called upon his God, JEHOVAH ELOHAY, to empower him to overcome his enemy.

Gideon gathered 32,000 men to help him fight the Midianites. But the Lord commanded Gideon to permit every man who was fearful to return home. Twenty-two thousand men accepted Gideon's offer. To Gideon's surprise, the Lord decided that 10,000 men were still too many. In a test given by God to determine the valiant, only 300 men qualified to fight the Midianites.

Gideon divided his army into three groups of 100 men each. Their meager weapons consisted only of lamps, pitchers, and trumpets! At Gideon's signal the men blew their trumpets, broke their pitchers, waved their torches, and shouted, " . . . *The sword of the LORD, and of Gideon"* (Judges 7:20). The panic-stricken Midianites suddenly began to attack and kill one another, and Gideon won the battle.

Perhaps you have felt inadequate for some task set before you, but like Gideon, when you call upon JEHOVAH ELOHAY, He will perform the miraculous for you.

Although Gideon called upon JEHOVAH ELOHAY and

rescued the people from their oppressors, the Israelites again lapsed into idolatry. In Judges 13, the Lord allowed the Philistines to seize the Israelites.

The Israelites remained captive for 40 years, but eventually God raised up a deliverer to free them from bondage. This deliverer was born to a man named Manoah and his wife. This couple desperately wanted a baby, but they were unable to conceive. One day an angel of the Lord appeared to Manoah's wife:

> . . . *Behold now, thou art barren, and bearest not: but thou shalt conceive, and bear a son . . . and no razor shalt come on his head: for the child shall be a Nazarite unto God from the womb: and he shall begin to deliver Israel out of the hand of the Philistines* (Judges 13:3,5).

Now this frightened Manoah. He realized that he and his wife were going to have a supernatural baby, and they needed divine guidance to raise him properly:

> *Then Manoah entreated the LORD, and said, 'O my Lord, let the man of God which thou didst send come again unto us, and teach us what we shall do unto the child that shall be born'* (Judges 13:8).

By calling upon "the Lord, **my** God," Manoah brought JEHOVAH ELOHAY into the situation and received an answer to his prayer:

> *"And God hearkened to the voice of Manoah; and*

*the angel of God came again . . . "* (Judges 13:9).

The angel instructed Manoah and his wife, and they raised their child, whom they named Samson, in strict Nazarite fashion. And Samson grew to be a strong man who accomplished many deeds for God. In one instance Samson used only the jawbone of an ass to massacre a thousand Philistines.

True, Samson was blessed with tremendous physical strength—but a moral weakness proved to be fatal: Samson did not have the moral tenacity to resist the charms of Delilah, the beautiful Philistine from Sorek; and she soon had him in her clutches.

As soon as Delilah learned that Samson's strength came from living a strict Nazarite lifestyle and from never cutting his hair, she double-crossed him and shared his secret with the Philistines. While Samson was sleeping, the Philistines cut his hair and gouged out his eyes. With his strength reduced to that of an ordinary man, Samson was easily subdued and sent to prison where he ground grain. When a feast day came, the Philistines brought him to their temple and ridiculed him. But in this desperate hour, Samson made a final petition to God:

*And Samson called unto the LORD, and said, O Lord GOD, remember me, I pray thee, and strengthen me, I pray thee, only this once, O God, that I may be at once avenged of the Philistines for my two eyes* (Judges 16:28).

Samson called upon JEHOVAH ELOHAY, "the Lord, **my** God," who endued him with mighty power. With a sudden burst of strength, Samson pushed over two pillars and brought the temple crashing down upon himself and his enemies:

*" . . . So the dead which he slew at his death were more than they which he slew in his life"* (Judges 16:30).

Yes, we can call upon JEHOVAH ELOHAY when we personally experience trials, but what should we do when we see a loved one—or even an enemy—experiencing fiery circumstances? Should we throw on another log and watch the flames really soar? No. We should call upon EL-ELOHE-ISRAEL, meaning "the personal God of Israel" to rescue that person from the destruction. We can replace the word *ISRAEL* with the name of the person for whom we are interceding. For example, if I am interceding for my husband, I can personalize my prayer by calling upon EL-ELOHE-WALLY, meaning "the personal God of Wally."

Jacob was the first man to call the Lord EL-ELOHE-ISRAEL. Jacob, meaning "the supplanter," went through many fiery trials—some of which occurred because of his own doing. But when he learned to call upon EL-ELOHE-ISRAEL, Jacob's circumstances were changed and his life was transformed.

Jacob mistreated his twin brother Esau by buying his birthright and stealing his blessing. Esau was so angry that he vowed to kill his brother. So Jacob fled to Haran to live with his Uncle Laban, who, as Jacob soon learned, far surpassed him in the art of treachery.

After several years of being cheated by Laban, the Lord appeared to Jacob in a dream and instructed him to return to his homeland. Now Jacob would be between two enemies: his Uncle Laban was behind him and his brother Esau was before him. Realizing his helplessness, Jacob began to pray:

*"Deliver me, I pray thee, . . ."* (Genesis 32:11).

That same night the angel of the Lord began to wrestle with Jacob who declared, *". . . I will not let thee go, except thou bless me"* (Genesis 32:26). It was dawn before the struggle ended. Finally, God announced, *". . . Thy name shall be called no more Jacob, but Israel: for as a prince hast thou power with God and with men, and hast prevailed"* (Genesis 32:28). Jacob, the "supplanter" was transformed into Israel, the "prince."

The newly named Israel may have survived his encounter with the Lord, but he still had to face his brother Esau who, along with 400 warriors, was traveling to meet him. In accordance with Mid-Eastern and Oriental custom, Jacob bowed seven times as he approached his brother. Esau ran to greet Israel and embraced and kissed him.

After their emotional reunion, Esau returned to his home in Mount Seir, and Israel continued his journey to Shechem. There he bought a parcel of land from the Hivite Hamor and erected an altar which he called EL-ELOHE-ISRAEL.

We all know people who are experiencing fiery trials. These people may be close friends or loved ones—or they may be enemies. But regardless of their position in our lives, it is our responsibility to petition EL-ELOHE-ISRAEL to rescue them from the flames:

*"And others save with fear, pulling them out of the fire; hating even the garment spotted by the flesh"* (Jude 23).

We've learned about JEHOVAH ELOHAY, Who is our personal God upon Whom we can call to deliver us from trials; and we've learned about EL-ELOHE-ISRAEL, upon Whom we can call to deliver others from fiery circumstances. But we need to call upon JEHOVAH ELOHEENU when the Body of Christ as a whole is under attack.

JEHOVAH ELOHEENU has proved many times that He is Lord to the corporate Body of Christ. It is wonderful when we pray to JEHOVAH ELOHAY and receive a personal miracle; but I have found that when I pray to JEHOVAH ELOHEENU and have faith for the *corporate* Body of Christ to receive a miracle, I begin to get the vision of the kingdom. I see what God can do in the world when we knit our hearts together in prayer toward a common goal.

For example, several years ago I wanted desperately to teach the Bible on educational television. It was absolutely a miracle that the station's president allowed us to air our program.

However, in an effort to cancel our program, a group of atheists picketed the station. At first I thought, "God, this is SO embarrassing! Why are You allowing this to happen?" And He reminded me that my work had to be tried with fire:

> *Every man's work shall be made manifest: for the day shall declare it, because it shall be revealed by fire; and the fire shall try every man's work of what sort it is* (I Corinthians 3:13).

Anything that survives God's fire will come out gold.

The station didn't respond to the atheists' protests, so they decided to argue their case before the public school board. The school board meeting took place on a Wednesday evening—which corresponded with our mid-week service. The atheists sent their best and most knowledgeable speaker to the board meeting. Our congregation agreed in prayer that no weapon formed against us would prosper and that the meeting would be put to confusion.

The superintendent of schools called upon the speaker to present the atheists' case. But the man's speech was confused, and he was even unable to pronounce his own name correctly. The superintendent asked, "Is there something wrong, sir?"

The speaker answered, "No, nothing is wrong."

But when he tried to present his case again, his speech was unintelligible. Finally, the superintendent said, "Sir, please sit down, and don't bother us with this case again."

We received a miracle that night because the people in our congregation caught hold of a vision that would bless the entire Body. Then they united their hearts in prayer, believing that JEHOVAH ELOHEENU would perform a miracle.

Moses had a corporate vision of the Israelites and the miracles that God wanted to perform for them. Do you think that Moses pastored the sweetest people in the world? No! I think he had the biggest bunch of murmurers I've ever heard about in my life! Yet Moses believed God to provide miracles for these people.

This was the key to Moses' life: he never gave up on the corporate miracle for the Hebrew nation. Whether the Israelites were nasty or nice, Moses still believed God to bless them.

In Exodus 24 Moses was summoned before God on the mount to receive the tablets of stone. Aaron and Hur were to assume leadership during Moses' absence:

> *"And Moses went into the midst of the cloud, and gat him up into the mount: and Moses was in the mount forty days and forty nights"* (Exodus 24:18).

However, while Moses was experiencing spiritual triumph, the Israelites were plummeting into new depths of spiritual decadence. They became fearful because of Moses' delay, so they went to Aaron and asked him to construct an object that they could follow. Aaron complied with their request:

> *And all the people brake off the golden earrings which were in their ears, and brought them unto Aaron. And he received them at their hand, and fashioned it with a graving tool, after he had made it a molten calf: and they said, These be thy gods, O Israel, which brought thee up out of the land of Egypt* (Exodus 32:3,4).

Aaron not only made the bull-calf, but he identified it with God:

> *"And when Aaron saw it, he built an altar before it; and Aaron made proclamation, and said, Tomorrow is a feast to the LORD'"* (Exodus 32:5).

The next day the people held a festival to the "LORD" and sacrificed burnt offerings to the molten image. Their activities led to immorality: they began to drink heavily and to dance before their new idol.

God told Moses that the people had become corrupt and "stiffnecked" and refused to claim the people as His own. God

279

wanted to punish the Israelites' rebellion by destroying them and using Moses to begin a new nation.

The Israelites had grumbled and complained throughout their journey. Furthermore they had blamed Moses for most of their misery. But Moses didn't want revenge. If I had been Moses, I might have said, "Good! They deserve it; let them have it!" But Moses had a corporate vision of the future of God's kingdom, and he wanted to do what was best for it as a whole. Moses pleaded with God to have mercy on the Israelites. Moses knew that God's testimony to the Egyptians would also be destroyed if He destroyed the Israelites. Would God, Who had promised to make the descendants of Abraham, Issac, and Jacob innumerable, and Who had promised to lead them to a land flowing with milk and honey, now become known as the God Who breaks His promises?

Moses' intercession saved the nation: God agreed not to destroy the entire population and sent Moses down the mountain to confront the people. Moses could barely believe the moral decay that had overtaken the Israelites. In anger, Moses smashed the stone tablets and burned the idol. After summoning Aaron to give an account of what had happened, Moses commanded the Levites—the only ones who had not participated in the rebellion—to search the camp and kill those who persisted in the idolatry.

However, Moses recognized that the nation as a whole shared the guilt; therefore, he ascended the mountain to intercede for the Israelites' sin. God told Moses that he and the people should continue to move toward the Promised Land, but that an angel, not God Himself, would accompany them on the journey. Why wouldn't God accompany them? Because He would be tempted to destroy them:

*"'. . . I will not go up in the midst of thee; for thou art a stiffnecked people: lest I consume thee in the way'"* (Exodus 33:3).

Now this was very serious! God would not rescind His promise to spare the Israelites; yet He still did not want to be associated with them. However, Moses would not give up. He continued his intercession to JEHOVAH ELOHEENU:

*Now therefore, I pray thee, if I have found grace in thy sight, shew me now thy way, that I may know thee, that I may find grace in thy sight: and consider that this nation is thy people* (Exodus 33:13).

Moses was bold! He intervened by reminding God that the Israelites were indeed His people. In response to Moses' prayer, the Lord reversed His threat and agreed to accompany the Hebrew nation to the Promised Land.

Would you like to have the same relationship with God as Moses had? Psalm 103:7 clearly reveals Moses' relationship with God: *"He made known his ways unto Moses, his acts unto the children of Israel."* The Israelites knew God only through His acts of power, but Moses knew God face to face.

We need to know God in all the aspects of His power—He is our Healer, Creator, and Deliverer. But we also must know God personally—as our Friend and adoring heavenly Father.

Take time every day to cultivate your relationship with JEHOVAH ELOHAY, "the Lord, **my** God." Allow Him to reveal His character and the essence of His being to you. As you grow in this relationship, soon you will be able to expand your faith to pray to EL-ELOHE-ISRAEL and assume an integral role in helping to relieve others' suffering. Finally, seriously consider your relationship with JEHOVAH ELOHEENU, "the Lord, **our** God." Allow Him to expand your vision to grasp His plan for the Body of Christ. You will be marvelously blessed as you receive answers to prayer for your church, your city, and even your nation.

## JEHOVAH ELOHAY

*And Joshua said, Alas, O **Lord** God, wherefore hast thou at all brought this people over Jordan, to deliver us into the hand of the Amorities, to destroy us? would to God we had been content, and dwelt on the other side Jordan! O **Lord**, what shall I say, when Israel turneth their backs before their enemies!* (Joshua 7:7,8).

*And he said unto him, Oh my **Lord**, wherewith shall I save Israel? behold, my family is poor in Manasseh, and I am the least in my father's house* (Judges 6:15).

*Then Manoah intreated the LORD, and said, O my **Lord**, let the man of God which thou didst send come again unto us, and teach us what we shall do unto the child that shall be born* (Judges 13:8).

*"O my soul, thou hast said unto the LORD, Thou art my **Lord**: my goodness extendeth not to thee"* (Psalms 16:2).

## EL-ELOHE-ISRAEL

*And Jacob came to Shalem, a city of Shechem, which is in the land of Canaan, when he came from Padan-aram; and pitched his tent before the city. And he bought a parcel of a field, where he had spread his tent, at the hand of the children of Hamor, Shechem's father, for an hundred pieces of money.*

*And he erected there an altar, and called it*
**El-elohe-Israel** (Genesis 33:18-20).

## JEHOVAH ELOHEENU

*The LORD our **God** spake unto us in Horeb,*
*saying, Ye have dwelt long enough in this mount.*
*And when we departed from Horeb, we went*
*through all that great and terrible wilderness, which*
*ye saw by the way of the mountain of the Amorites,*
*as the LORD our **God** commanded us; and we came*
*to Kadesh-barnea. And I said unto you, Ye are come*
*unto the mountain of the Amorites, which the LORD*
*our **God** doth give unto us* (Deuteronomy 1:6,19,20).

*And the LORD our **God** delivered him before us;*
*and we smote him, and his sons, and all his people.*
*From Aroer, which is by the brink of the river of*
*Arnon, and from the city that is by the river, even*
*unto Gilead, there was not one city too strong for*
*us: the LORD our **God** delivered all unto us*
(Deuteronomy 2:33,36).

*And ye said, Behold, the LORD our **God** hath*
*shewed us his glory and his greatness, and we have*
*heard his voice out of the midst of the fire: we have*
*seen this day that God doth talk with man, and he*
*liveth* (Deuteronomy 5:24).

*"Hear, O Israel: The LORD our **God** is one LORD"*
(Deuteronomy 6:4).

*The secret things belong unto the LORD our **God**: but those things which are revealed belong unto us and to our children for ever, that we may do all the words of this law* (Deuteronomy 29:29).

# Receive Jesus Christ as Lord and Savior of Your Life.

The Bible says, "That if thou shalt confess with thy mouth the Lord Jesus, and shalt believe in thine heart that God hath raised him from the dead, thou shalt be saved. For with the heart man believeth unto righteousness; and with the mouth confession is made unto salvation" (Romans 10:9,10).

To receive Jesus Christ as Lord and Savior of your life, sincerely pray this prayer from your heart:

Dear Jesus,

I believe that You died for me and that You rose again on the third day. I confess to You that I am a sinner and that I need Your love and forgiveness. Come into my life, forgive my sins, and give me eternal life. I confess You now as my Lord. Thank You for my salvation!

Signed _____

Date _____

## Write to us.
We will send you information to help you with your new life in Christ.

Marilyn Hickey Ministries • P.O. Box 17340
Denver, CO 80217 • (303) 770-0400

## BOOKS BY MARILYN HICKEY

A CRY FOR MIRACLES ($5.95)
ACTS ($7.95)
ANGELS ALL AROUND ($7.95)
BEAT TENSION ($.75)
BIBLE CAN CHANGE YOU, THE ($12.95)
BOLD MEN WIN ($.75)
BREAK THE GENERATION CURSE ($7.95)
BULLDOG FAITH ($.75)
CHANGE YOUR LIFE ($.75)
CHILDREN WHO HIT THE MARK ($.75)
CONQUERING SETBACKS ($.75)
DAILY DEVOTIONAL ($5.95)
DEAR MARILYN ($5.95)
DIVORCE IS NOT THE ANSWER ($4.95)
ESPECIALLY FOR TODAY'S WOMAN ($14.95)
EXPERIENCE LONG LIFE ($.75)
FASTING & PRAYER ($.75)
FREEDOM FROM BONDAGES ($4.95)
GIFT-WRAPPED FRUIT ($2.00)
GOD'S BENEFIT: HEALING ($.75)
GOD'S COVENANT FOR YOUR FAMILY ($5.95)
GOD'S RX FOR A HURTING HEART ($3.50)
GOD'S SEVEN KEYS TO MAKE YOU RICH ($.75)
HOLD ON TO YOUR DREAM ($.75)
HOW TO BE A MATURE CHRISTIAN ($5.95)
HOW TO BECOME MORE THAN A CONQUEROR ($.75)
HOW TO WIN FRIENDS ($.75)
I CAN BE BORN AGAIN AND SPIRIT FILLED ($.75)
I CAN DARE TO BE AN ACHIEVER ($.75)
KEYS TO HEALING REJECTION ($.75)
KNOW YOUR MINISTRY ($3.50)
MAXIMIZE YOUR DAY . . . GOD'S WAY ($7.95)
NAMES OF GOD ($7.95)
#1 KEY TO SUCCESS—MEDITATION, THE ($3.50)
POWER OF FORGIVENESS, THE ($.75)
POWER OF THE BLOOD, THE ($.75)
RECEIVING RESURRECTION POWER ($.75)
RENEW YOUR MIND ($.75)
SATAN-PROOF YOUR HOME ($7.95)
"SAVE THE FAMILY" PROMISE BOOK ($14.95)
SIGNS IN THE HEAVENS ($5.95)
SOLVING LIFE'S PROBLEMS ($.75)
SPEAK THE WORD ($.75)
STANDING IN THE GAP ($.75)
STORY OF ESTHER, THE ($.75)
WINNING OVER WEIGHT ($.75)
WOMEN OF THE WORD ($.75)
YOUR MIRACLE SOURCE ($3.50)
YOUR PERSONALITY WORKOUT ($5.95)